YOUR STATE IN CROSS-STITCH

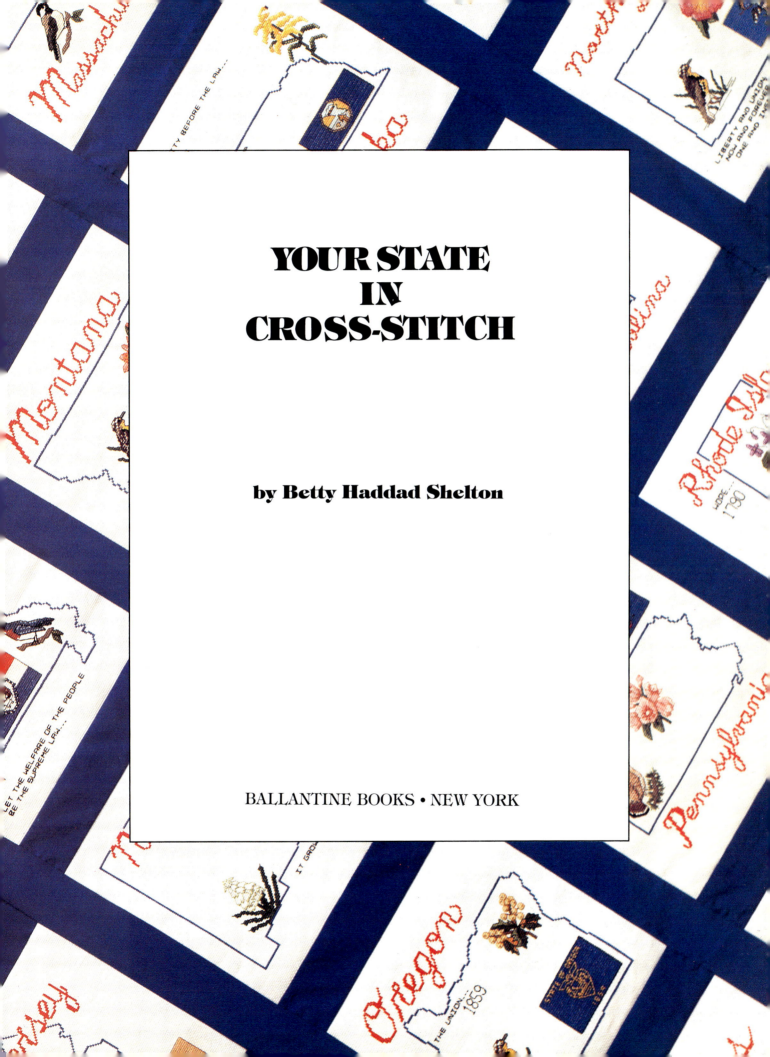

YOUR STATE IN CROSS-STITCH

by Betty Haddad Shelton

BALLANTINE BOOKS • NEW YORK

Ad Majorem Gloriam Dei

To my son Jeffrey Michael, my help, my heart, my pride, my joy.

Produced for Ballantine Books
by TENTH AVENUE EDITIONS, INC.

Text and Notes by Clare Johnson

Managing Editor: Clive Giboire
Executive Editor: Patricia Ann Higgins
Associate Editors: Jayne Arden
  and Suzanne Gagné
Art Directors: Gilda Hannah
  and Walter Skibitsky
Graphic Artist: Patrick O'Brien
Photographer: George Roos

Photographs, half title and title
pages, Eastern Studios; page 100,
Myron Miller

Copyright © 1987 by Betty Haddad Shelton
All rights reserved under International and Pan-American
Copyright Conventions. Published in the United States by
Ballantine Books, a division of Random House, Inc., New York, and
simultaneously in Canada by Random House of Canada Limited,
Toronto.

Library of Congress Catalog Card Number: 86-92105

ISBN: 0-345-34635-1

Cover design by James R. Harris
Manufactured in the United States of America
First Edition: September 1987

1
INTRODUCTION

5
GENERAL INSTRUCTIONS

Materials

Preparation

The Stitches

7
YOUR STATE

Washington D.C. followed by
the 50 states in alphabetical order

100
FINISHING

Mounting and Framing

Pillow Instructions

Quilt Instructions

Resources

ACKNOWLEDGEMENTS

The editors acknowledge with gratitude the assistance of these individuals, state officials, and agencies who provided valuable information on the state symbols discussed in this book: Alabama State Department of Archives and History, Montogomery, Alabama; David G. Koivuniemi, Office of the LieutenantGovernor, Juneau, Alaska; Arizona Highways Magazine, Phoenix, Arizona; W.J. McCuen, Secretary of State, Little Rock, Arkansas; March Fong Eu, Secretary of State, Sacremento, California; Office of the Secretary of State, Denver, Colorado; Julia H. Tashjian, Secretary of State, Hartford, Connecticut; Delaware State Travel Service, Dover, Delaware; George Firestone, Secretary of State, Tallahassee, Florida; Max Cleland, Secretary of State, Atlanta, Georgia; Keola Beamer, Office of the Lieutenant Governor, Honolulu, Hawaii; Office of the Secretary of State, Boise, Idaho; Jim Edgar, Secretary of State, Springfield, Illinois; Velvet C. Short, Office of the Secretary of State, Indianapolis, Indiana; Paulee Lipsman, Office of the Secretary of State, Des Moines, Iowa; Jack H. Brier, Secretary of State, Topeka, Kansas; Ruth C. Thompson, Department of Travel Development, Frankfort, Kentucky; James H. Brown, Secretary of State, Baton Rouge, Louisiana; Office ofthe Secretary of State, Annapolis, Maryland; Carol Rosen, Office of the Secretary of State, Boston, Massachusetts; Richard Austin, Secretary of State, Lansing, Michigan; Joan Anderson Growe, Secretary of State, St. Paul, Minnesota; Dick Molpus, Secretary of State, Jackson, Mississippi; Roy D. Blunt, Secretary of State, Jefferson City, Missouri; Jim Waltermire, Secretary of State, Helena, Montana; Allen J. Beerman, Secretary of State, Lincoln, Nebraska; Richard F. Moreno, Nevada Commission on Tourism, Carson City, Nevada; Office of the Secretary of State, Portsmouth, New Hampshire; Clara P. Jones, Secretary of State, Albuquerque, New Mexico; Office of the Secretary of State, Albany, New York; Thad Eure, Secretary of State, Raleigh, North Carolina; Ben Meier, Secretary of State, Bismarck, North Dakota; Sherrod Brown, Secretary of State, Columbus, Ohio; Karen Stanton Fife, Oklahoma Department of Libraries, Oklahoma City, Oklahoma; Barbara Roberts, Secretary of State, Salem, Oregon; Office of the Secretary of State, Harrisburg, Pennsylvania; Henry S. Kinch, Office of the Secretary of State, Providence, Rhode Island; Joyce Hazeltine, Secretary of State, Pierre, South Dakota; Gentry Crowell, Secretary of State, Nashville, Tennessee; John Reigler, Office of the Secretary of State, Austin, Texas; Janet Davey, Office of the Secretary of State, Salt Lake City, Utah; James H. Douglas, Secretary of State, Montpelier, Vermont; Martha W. Steger, Department of Economic Development, Richmond, Virginia; Ralph Munro, Secretary of State, Olympia, Washington; Ken Hechler, Secretary of State, Charleston, West Virginia; William H. Barton, Wyoming State Archives, Museums and Historical Department, Cheyenne, Wyoming.

INTRODUCTION

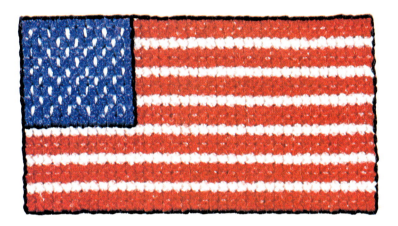

The states' flags exemplify the diversity that was and is the essence of these United States. They have developed their symbolism from a complex mix of early United States history, topography, inspiration, and coincidence.

The 13 colonies drafted the Articles of Confederation in 1777. In the words of James Madison, these Articles were "nothing more than an alliance between independent and sovereign states." Under them, the states maintained their own currencies, tariffs, and, in several instances, their own navies. In 1787, the United States Constitution was ratified six years after the War of Independence had been fought and won in 1781. Only then did the colonies become truly united.

Perhaps no other people in history have so strongly identified with their flags as have Americans. Even our national anthem was written about our flag. So fervently was that flag venerated during the Civil War that waving Old Glory was considered a sign of patriotism, and showing disrespect to it was considered treason. Despite a profound sense of "one nation, indivisible," the states' populations also had an historical sense of themselves, and so state flags were also created.

These flags are a glorious crazy quilt of colors and emblems. In their variety, the flags reflect that sense of local identity that goes hand in hand with Americans' sense of, and pride in, their national identity.

The states' flags are rich in symbols peculiar and unique to them. Their devices range from native American symbolism and feudal heraldry to uncluttered modernity, from Confederate vestiges to florid Victoriana, from the English and revolutionary French red, white, and blue to Isabella of Castille's colors, and from 18th-century symbols of liberty to 19th-century symbols of idealized materialism.

State flags present a panoply of contradictions and contrasts. There is a 172-year gap between the ratification of the Constitution by the first of the original 13 colonies in 1787, and the entry into the Union of the two states admitted in 1959, Alaska and Hawaii. Moreover, the addition of states did not progress in stepwise, chronological order from east to west across the continent. Certain western states were added to the Union before other more eastern territories because, during the Civil War, the Union needed their precious metals to finance the war.

After the Civil War, as more and more states were added to the Union, Iowa's legislature resisted the adoption af an individual state flag, for to do so seemed disrespectful to the national flag. There, the lobbying efforts of the veterans of the Grand Army of the Republic prevailed: when the present state emblem was adopted in 1921, it was referred to by law, not as a flag, but as a *banner*.

Symbolism served the needs of preliterate societies. For them, its shorthand pictures were worth, indeed, any number of words. New Mexico's flag bears perhaps the oldest form of symbolism, and certainly the oldest native American symbolism, found on a state's flag. It depicts in centered simplicity the pre-Columbian sun symbol of the Zia Pueblo: this is ancient symbolism indeed.

Even heraldry, an antique, European form of family and national symbolism, is still sometimes seen in its pure form among the state flags. Heraldic conventions were the symbols used by feudal Europe's preliterate societies. The evolved, true coat of arms, with its crest, supporters, shield, and motto is found on 11 state flags. (The motto was an additional device employed when sufficient numbers of the European aristocracy had learned to read.) Such heraldic conventions as cresents and stars denote second sons.

One state flag that is purely heraldic is that of Maryland, which bears the quartered arms of Lord Baltimore's 17th-century English families, the Crosslands and the Calverts. Among others are Alabama's simple cross of St. Andrew on a pure white field, Connecticut's straightforward 17th-century shield, and Washington D.C.'s use of General George Washington's old English family arms.

The flags' most common emblem is the five-pointed star, but, in 1776, it had not been used on the flag of any nation. Such stars were a relatively uncommon heraldic convention used by second sons; significantly, George Washington's ancestors employed them. Today, five-pointed stars appear on the national flag and on 19 state flags, in rings, in rows, even in a constellation (California). We have made stars our own, and placed them on the flags in white, yellow, silver, gold, and copper.

The District of Columbia flag adopted in 1938 draws upon the shield granted to Lawrence Washington of Sulgraave Manor, Northamptonshire, England, in 1592. Sulgrave Manor was President George Washington's ancestral seat. The three red five-pointed stars, derived from the Washington family's English shield, appear to represent the three branches of the United States Government: legislative, executive, and judicial. But the stars and the two broad red stripes running horizontally across the white field come from 16th-century England, a time and place where neither the United States nor the federal government that Washington D.C. represents existed.

Many of the flags use the colors carried by their state militias. For most of U. S. history, blue has been the color of the country's infantry; most of the troops that fought against the British under General George Washington wore blue with facings—uniform collars, cuffs and lapels—of some contrasting color. Several of the oldest states chose the facing colors, rather than the uniform

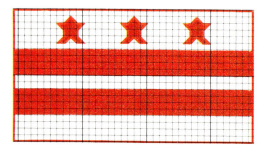

Flag of the District of Columbia, cross-stitched original (top), chart (bottom). Use white and 321

colors, of the state militias as their flags' background. Many flags still show their military derivation, but North Dakota's is the only one to survive exactly as carried by its militia.

Most states, however, did not enter the Union until after the beginning of the 19th century, when the blue of Washington's day had been adopted by the infantry of the United States Army. It then became convenient to use the many newly designed state seals, on their blue fields, to serve as the new state flags.

Because the Founding Fathers and their state and national governmental successors were literate, the state flags are among the wordiest in the world. Only Muslims, whose faith denies them the use of divine images, are more dependent on words for their flags.

The flags of the first 13 states do show restraint in their use of words. Those that use any words at all limit them to a simple, brief motto or an important date.

A majority (31) of the states, however, entered the Union during the 19th century, when the desire to show off their populations' increasing literacy was so strongly felt that some designers put words into almost every available open space—not just mottoes, but dates, slogans, nicknames, adjectives, and nouns describing the states' virtues and aspirations.

This abundance of words made for very crowded state seals, and for flags that were so expensive to stitch that some states eventually dispensed with using their seal as a device. A refreshing example of such practicality involves the design of Washington state's flag—the designer rejected a complicated seal and replaced it with George Washington's image, which was taken right from a postage stamp, and encircled by a dark green ground.

The increasingly literate state populations also became increasingly industrial, and tools became emblems of this new, industrialized America. The steamboat, perhaps the most popular symbol of 19th-century progress, outnumbers the steam locomotive four to two, for navigable waterways were more abundant than railroads and far less expensive to maintain. Agricultural and mining tools were also used—the plow is pictured on ten state flags; the miner's pick is featured on six.

Because they were characterized by vast tracts of wilderness, the states often depicted animals on their flags. The animals—some fierce, some placid, most indigenous—generally serve as supporters of crests or shields. But the grizzly bear of California, the beaver of Oregon, the bison of Wyoming, the pelican of Louisiana, and the eagles of Illinois, Iowa, and North Dakota serve as central devices. Although all the animals serving as central devices are wild and indigenous, New Jersey and Pennsylvania feature the useful, agrarian horse cresting and supporting, respectively, their state shields.

The American eagle is featured prominently on the flags of eight states and is central on three. North Dakota's flag is dominated by an eagle at its center, displaying spread wings, carrying an olive branch in its right talon and a clutch of 13 arrows in its left talon. The eagle's breast is formed by the shield of the United States. In its beak it holds the motto of the United States, *E Pluribus Unum*, and above its head in two semicircular rows are 13 golden stars, surmounted by a golden sunburst.

On Illinois's flag the eagle stands triumphant and alert, with wings outstretched, ready to fly. In its talons is clutched the red, white, and blue shield of the United States, and in its beak a red ribbon unfurls the phrases "National Union" and "State Sovereignty."

On the flag of Iowa a rather more serene eagle, shown in

The state seal of New Hampshire (top). Official flag of California (bottom)

flight, carries in its beak a very long blue ribbon inscribed with the words of the state motto, "Our Liberties We Prize and Our Rights We Will Maintain."

In the old days, when state flags were hand-stitched, or in some cases painted, only a few existed even in the states they represented. The precious hand-stitched objects were often one of a kind. Sales volume and cost efficiency did not have the importance that they have today, and many flags had two designs, one for each side of the flag. But now that flags are on demand for public buildings and businesses, cost matters, and so only one flag still has a separate design on its reverse side: the large golden beaver that appears on the reverse side of the flag of Oregon.

The flags have various dimensions: the broadest in relationship to height is Hawaii's flag at 2:1; the District of Columbia's is similar at 9:5. Alabama's, at 1:1, is square—as was the Battle Flag of the Confederacy. Twenty-one flags adopted the ratio of 3:2, breadth to height. Ohio flies the only burgee, that is, swallow-tail shaped flag.

The states' diversity is evidenced not only by their flags, but also, to a lesser extent, by the birds and flowers that they have chosen to represent them. The contiguous 48 states (2,966,625 square miles of land, 59,320 square miles of water, and over 20 degrees of longitude) have an enormous variety of climates and topographies, which is vastly expanded by the inclusion of Hawaii and Alaska. They provide an immense span of ecologies suitable for innumerable birds and flowers.

School children voted, and garden clubs and amateur ornithologists lobbied, often acrimoniously, for favorite birds and flowers to represent their states, but the final arbiters were the state legislatures. Their final decisions reflected the popular will, more appropriately in some cases than in others. One deadlocked state legislature actually flipped a coin to select its state flower.

One would expect the bird and flower symbols adopted by the individual states to have been chosen according to the species' prevalence within the state. More often than not this is the case; but birds are among the most mobile of living creatures, and flowers have broad ecologies as well. Indeed, they have been chosen as much for their beauty and popularity as for any specific physical attachments to states.

The cardinal is easily the most popular, and is the state bird of seven states; the meadowlark was adopted by six states; the bluebird represents five; the mockingbird was chosen by four—these four species, in other words, represent almost half the states in the Union. The robin, surprisingly, was chosen by only two states.

The states' flowers are more varied and specific than are their birds. Some variety of the rose, either in wild or cultivated form, has been chosen by four states—Georgia, Iowa, New York, and North Dakota—and the rhododendron represents Washington, West Virginia, and Wisconsin. The blossoms of fruit trees serve as symbols for four states. Oddly enough, Georgia adopted the Cherokee rose, and Delaware adopted the peach blossom. Mistletoe, the primeval oak-borne brightener of winter, is claimed by Oklahoma.

The state flags and symbols are in a very real sense the fabric of American life: plentious blue, red, and white and lots of earth colors, touches of Spanish crimson, the native Americans' colors, George Washington's stars and the buff of his uniform's facings, and the brilliant evergreen of Washington state. All the variety of America is represented.

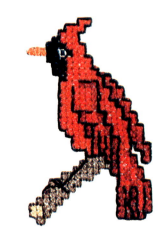

The cardinal (top), adopted by 7 states as their state bird. Peach blossom (bottom), State Flower of Delaware

GENERAL INSTRUCTIONS

MATERIALS

Cotton aida cloth was used throughout this book. When stitching on 14-count fabric, the embroidered area will measure about 7¼" by 7¾"; on 11-count, about 9¼" by 10"; on 18-count, about 5¾" by 6"; and on 22-count 4¾" by 5"

Use small, blunt tapestry needles, Nos. 24, 25, or 26.

All colors referred to are DMC Embroidery Floss. When working on 11- or 14-count fabric, use two strands of floss unless instructed otherwise. When 18- or 22-count fabric is used for background, use 1 strand throughout.

USE 797 FOR STATE OUTLINE AND 321 FOR STATE NAME THROUGHOUT.

A wooden or plastic embroidery hoop with a screw-type tension adjuster is essential as are sharp embroidery scissors.

PREPARATION

Cut 14-count fabric to measure 12" by 12". For other sizes, cut to allow 2" on all edges around embroidery. To prevent ravelling, either whipstitch or machine stitch around the outer edges of the fabric.

Locate the center of the fabric by folding it in half first vertically, then horizontally; the center stitch of the fabric falls where the creases meet. Mark the center with basting thread. Determine the center of the design, then count the number of stitches to the top of the design. Count on the fabric the same number of stitches above the center stitch. Mark with basting thread.

Place fabric in hoop and stretch tight. Beginning at top of piece, begin to work. Cut thread into about 18" lengths to help avoid knotting, twisting and fraying the thread while working. Always separate individual strands of thread before you begin to stitch. This will ensure better coverage. Thread has a nap and can be felt to be smoother in one direction. Always work with the nap (the smooth side should point down as your needle enters the fabric).

Take care to keep your hands immaculate while working to avoid stains on the cloth. Wash your hands frequently while working and dust your hands lightly with talcum or baby powder to prevent perspiration stains. Be sure to remove your embroidery from the hoop each time you stop stitching to prevent hoop marks from soiling your fabric. Store your work in a bag or basket to protect it from dust and spills, etc., when not being stitched.

THE STITCHES

To begin, fasten thread with a waste knot and anchor the thread with the first few stitches (see Figure 1). To begin, bring needle up through a hole in the fabric, cross the intersection, right and up on the diagonal and push needle down (see Figure 2). Continue across with first half of all the same-color stitches in a row. Next, cross back, right to left (see Figure 3).

Some needleworkers prefer to cross each stitch as they work. If using this method, care must be taken to make sure the top crosses are all slanting in the same direction.

Try to work from an open space to a filled space. Coming up in a space already stitched can cause "ruffling" of the previous stitch. Do not carry thread across an open area of fabric, as it will show when the piece is done.

To fasten off, weave the thread through the back of the stitches (see Figure 4).

To work a French knot, draw up needle through fabric, wrap thread around needle twice (see Figure 5), insert needle next to hole from which it came.

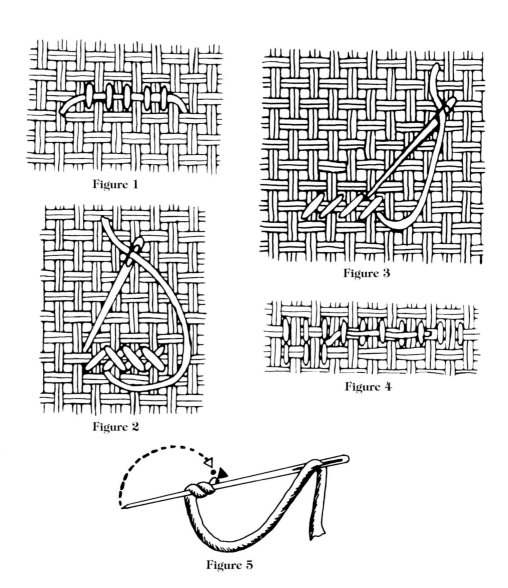

Figure 1

Figure 2

Figure 3

Figure 4

Figure 5

YOUR STATE

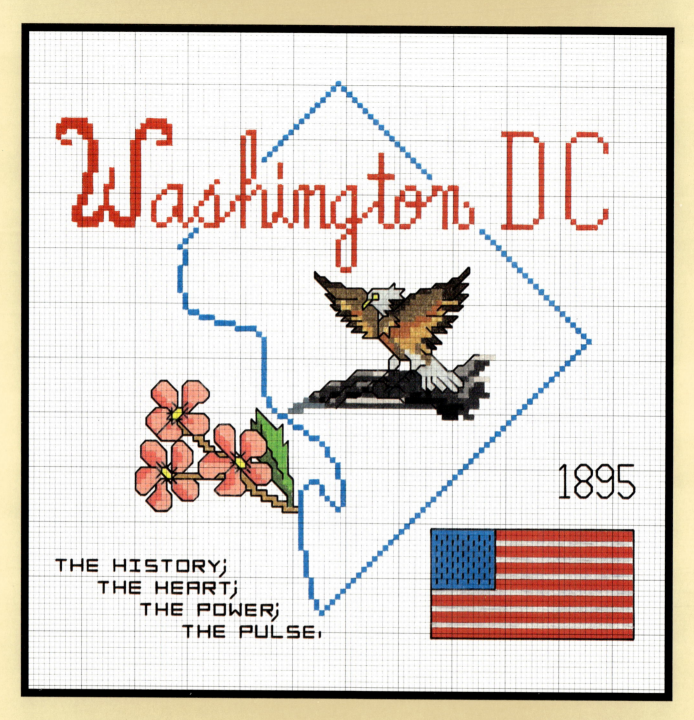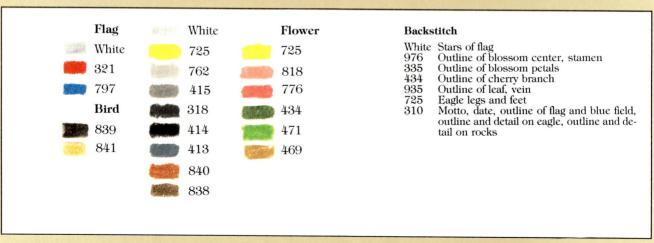

WASHINGTON, D.C.

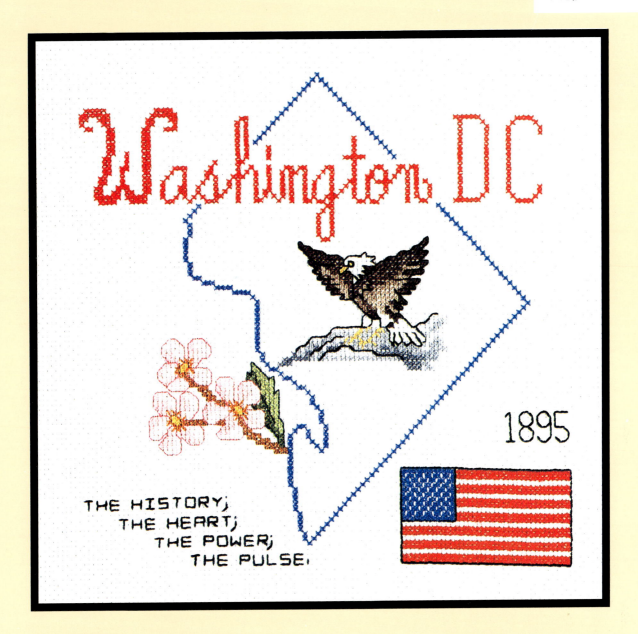

Established:	1791
Bird:	Bald eagle
Flower:	Cherry blossom
Nickname:	Seat of Government
	Nation's Capital

The city of Washington, coextensive with the District of Columbia, was established as the nation's capital as a compromise between North and South by acts of Congress in 1790 and 1791. Land was ceded by Virginia and Maryland for the new capital. Congress first met there in 1800. The city developed slowly (it was sacked by the British in the War of 1812). In 1889, plans for the city drawn up at President Washington's request by Pierre Charles L'Enfant a century earlier were exumed from the archives, and the city was developed in 1901 according to his plans.

On June 14, 1777, the Continental Congress adopted the 13-star, 13-stripe national flag, the basic design that is used today. Since the details of the design were not legally standardized, many variations were flown. Stars were arranged in circles and rows, with stars of from four to eight points. In 1794, a new flag was legislated, with 15 stripes and 15 stars (for the addition of two new states, Vermont and Kentucky). This is the flag that inspired Francis Scott Keyes when he wrote the "Star-Spangled Banner." In 1818, new legislation set the number of stripes to remain at 13 to represent the original 13 states, and provided for the addition of a star for every new state, to be added to the flag on the July 4th following the states' admission. Finally, in 1912, President Taft—by executive orders—established exact specifications.

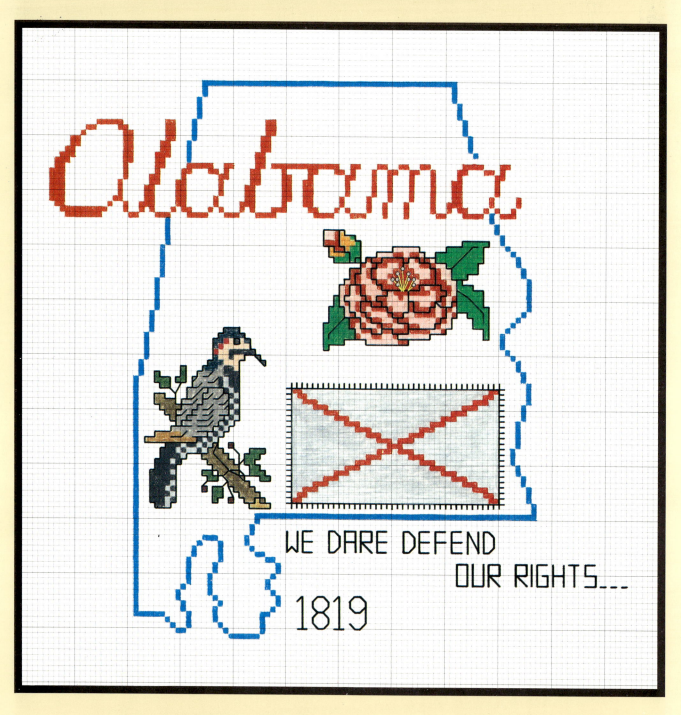

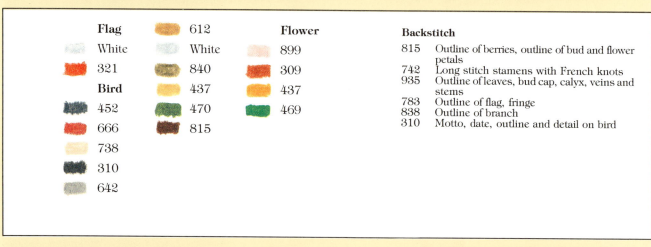

Flag		**Flower**		**Backstitch**	
White	612	899		815	Outline of berries, outline of bud and flower petals
321	White	309		742	Long stitch stamens with French knots
Bird	840	437		935	Outline of leaves, bud cap, calyx, veins and stems
452	437	469		783	Outline of flag, fringe
666	470			838	Outline of branch
738	815			310	Motto, date, outline and detail on bird
310					
642					

ALABAMA

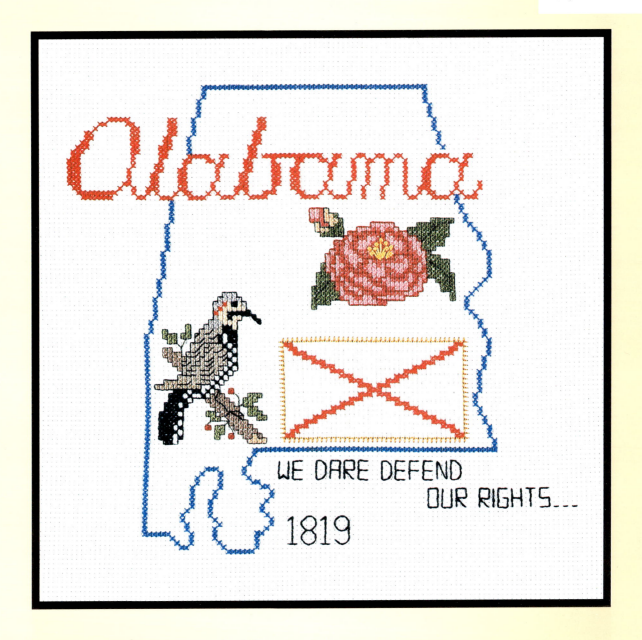

Entered Union: December 14, 1819
22nd state
Bird: Yellowhammer
Flower: Camellia
Nicknames: Cotton State
Yellowhammer State
Lizard State
Heart of Dixie

Alabama is one of the five states of the old South that boast flags strongly reminiscent of the Battle Flag of the Confederacy, with its white cross saltire of St. Andrew on red, overlaid with crossed blue bars and white stars. (The others are Arkansas, Florida, Georgia, and Mississippi.) Alabama remembers her past with her motto and also with her flag.

    The Alabama flag was adopted at the end of the 19th century, when memories of spilled Confederate blood found clear expression in the crimson cross on a field of pure white. In fact, when the flag is made according to its official dimensions, it exactly duplicates the dimensions of the Confederate Battle Flag (Stars and Bars), which was square rather than rectangular.

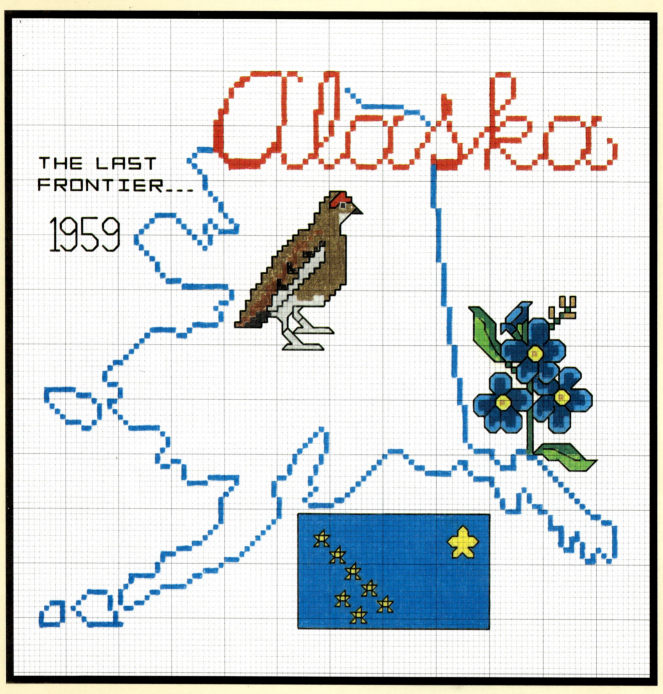

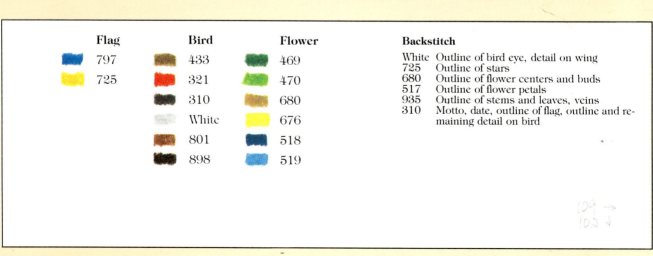

Flag	Bird	Flower	Backstitch	
797	433	469	White	Outline of bird eye, detail on wing
725	321	470	725	Outline of stars
	310	680	680	Outline of flower centers and buds
	White	676	517	Outline of flower petals
	801	518	935	Outline of stems and leaves, veins
	898	519	310	Motto, date, outline of flag, outline and remaining detail on bird

ALASKA

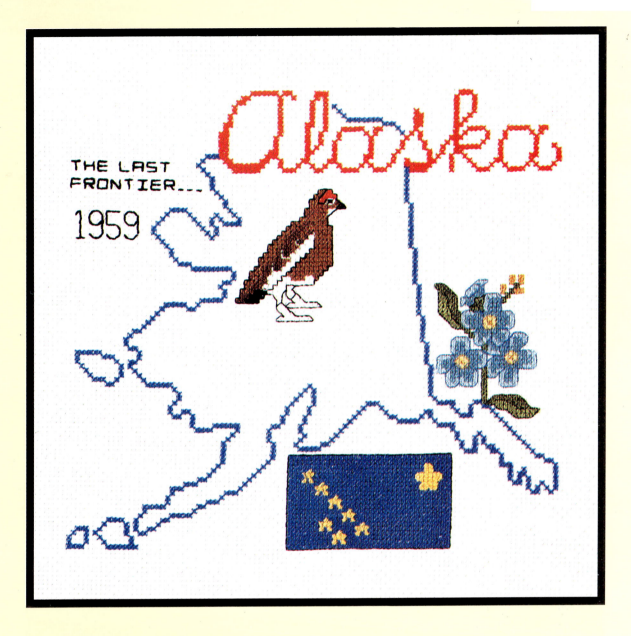

Entered Union:	January 3, 1959
	49th state
Bird:	Willow ptarmigan
Flower:	Forget-me-not
Nicknames:	The Last Frontier
	Land of the Midnight Sun
	America's Icebox

The simplicity and symbolic strength of Alaska's flag are the vision of a 13-year-old native Alaskan, Benny Benson. In 1926, this schoolboy won a contest held to select a flag for the territory. He received $1,000 for his design and, upon finishing school, he became an airplane mechanic.

With only two colors, blue and gold, the flag expresses the most powerful of Alaska's symbols. The blue field represents not only the huge sea and sky of Alaska, but also the forget-me-not, the state flower. The gold Ursa Major (the Big Dipper), aligned with Polaris (the North Star), reminds us not only of the most northern "star" of the Union, but of that precious metal which gave Alaska her first great population boost.

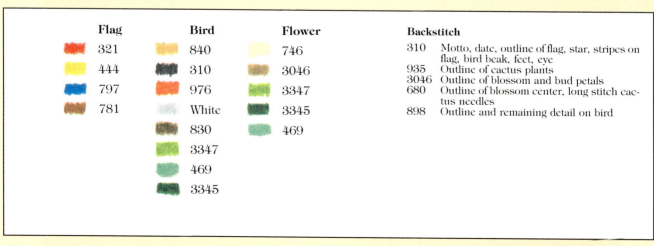

ARIZONA

Entered Union: February 19, 1912
48th state
Bird: Cactus wren
Flower: Saguaro cactus blossom
Nicknames: Grand Canyon State
Apache State

The spectacular splendor of nature in the Grand Canyon State is manifested in the state flag of Arizona. On it, a blazing sunrise with 13 rays of alternating red and golden-yellow mimicks the colors of the flag of imperial Spain. That flag was first brought by Coronado into what is now Arizona. The sunburst rises over a copper star set on a blue horizon—copper for the metal that gave Arizona so much wealth, and a star to recall the state motto, *Ditat Deus* (God Enriches).

At the time of the adoption of the Arizona flag in 1917, there was some controversy about the flag's sunburst being too reminiscent of the Rising Sun design used as a battle ensign by imperial Japan. The battleship, the *U.S.S. Arizona,* was presented with one of the first of the flags. Ironically and tragically, she was sunk at Pearl Harbor.

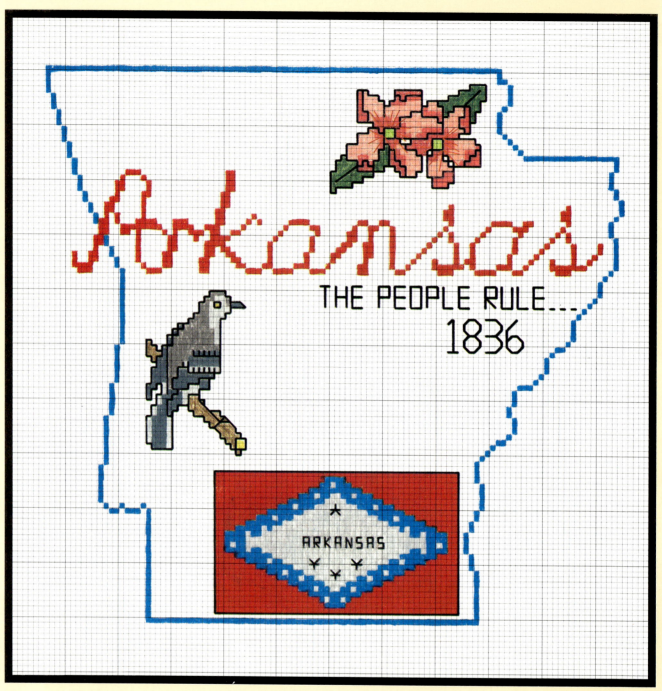

Flag	Bird	Flower	Backstitch	
■ 321	■ 414	■ 472	797	Stars on white field, "ARKANSAS" (3 strands)
■ 797	■ 437	■ 776	838	Outline of branch
□ White	■ 413	■ 818	335	Outline of flower petals
	White	■ 3052	741	Long stitch stamen with French knots
	■ 840		3052	Outline of leaves
			472	Leaf veins
			310	Motto, date, outline of flag, outline and remaining detail on bird

ARKANSAS

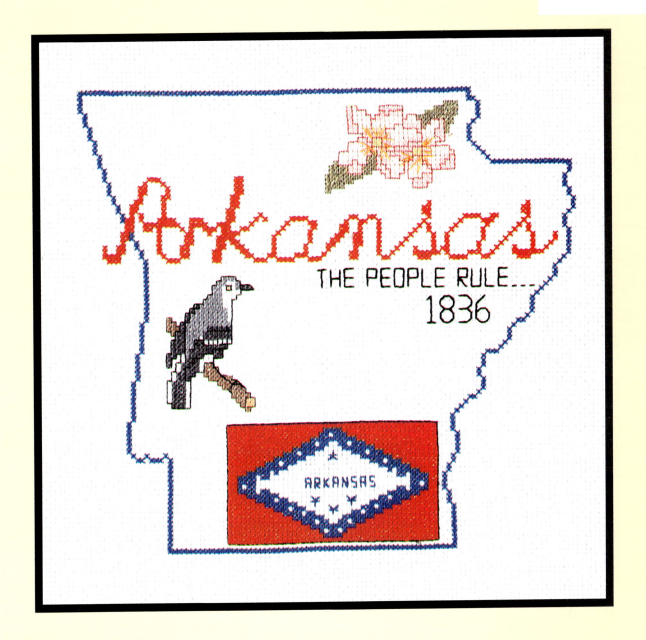

Entered Union: June 15, 1836
25th state
Bird: Mockingbird
Flower: Apple blossom
Nicknames: Wonder State
Land of Opportunity

The red, white and blue in the state flag of Arkansas seem to have an obvious significance. But the diamond bordered by blue bars with white stars centered on a red field gives a very real resemblance to the Confederate Battle Flag. Three blue stars below the state name inside the diamond symbolize DeSoto's discovery of the territory in 1541; the French claim, dating from 1686; and the the purchase of the territory from France in 1803 as part of the Louisiana Purchase. The fourth star, in the top half of the diamond, was added in 1923 out of respect for the Confederacy.

Arkansas, Land of Opportunity, is the only state in the Union to mine diamonds.

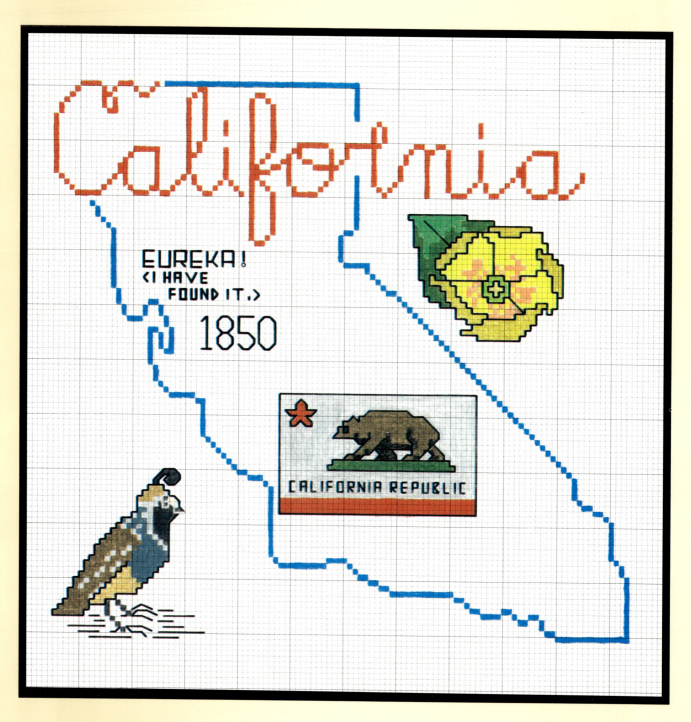

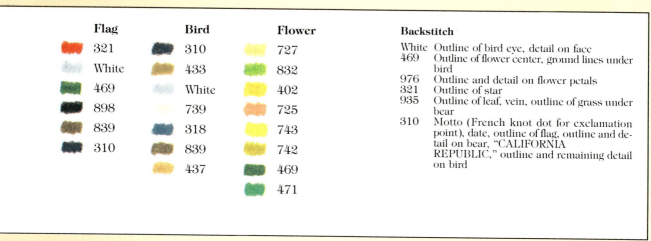

Flag	Bird	Flower	Backstitch	
321	310	727	White	Outline of bird eye, detail on face
White	433	832	469	Outline of flower center, ground lines under bird
469	White	402	976	Outline and detail on flower petals
898	739	725	321	Outline of star
839	318	743	935	Outline of leaf, vein, outline of grass under bear
310	839	742	310	Motto (French knot dot for exclamation point), date, outline of flag, outline and detail on bear, "CALIFORNIA REPUBLIC," outline and remaining detail on bird
	437	469		
		471		

CALIFORNIA

Entered Union: September 9, 1850
31st state
Bird: California valley quail
Flower: Golden poppy
Nickname: Golden State

The state flag of California has true grass-roots origins. Its basic design has survived since the mid-19th century. In 1846, American frontiersmen rose against the Mexican rulers of California and captured the Mexican garrison at Sonoma. A flag was improvised on the spot using strips of red cloth and white cloth from the skirts of local women. On it, a fierce California grizzly bear and the slogan "California Republic" were crudely painted.

The flag of the new "republic" flew over Sonoma for little over a month, when U. S. troops entered the area and declared it part of the United States. Upon entry into the Union in 1850, the new state retained the battle-seasoned Sonoma design. The original flag survived until 1906, when it was destroyed in the San Francisco fire.

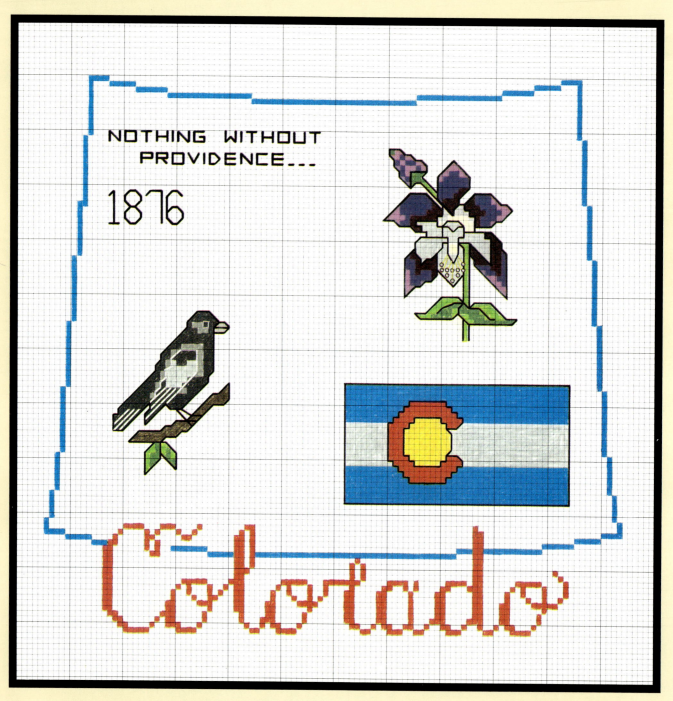

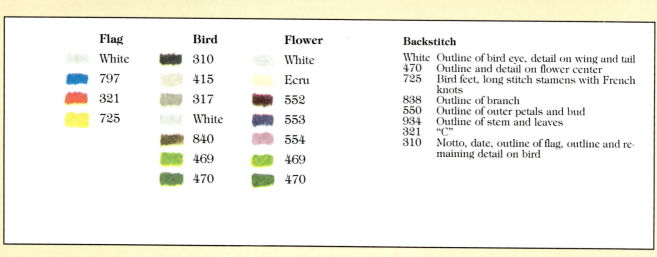

Flag	Bird	Flower	Backstitch	
White	310	White	White	Outline of bird eye, detail on wing and tail
797	415	Ecru	470	Outline and detail on flower center
321	317	552	725	Bird feet, long stitch stamens with French knots
725	White	553	838	Outline of branch
	840	554	550	Outline of outer petals and bud
	469	469	934	Outline of stem and leaves
	470	470	321	"C"
			310	Motto, date, outline of flag, outline and remaining detail on bird

COLORADO

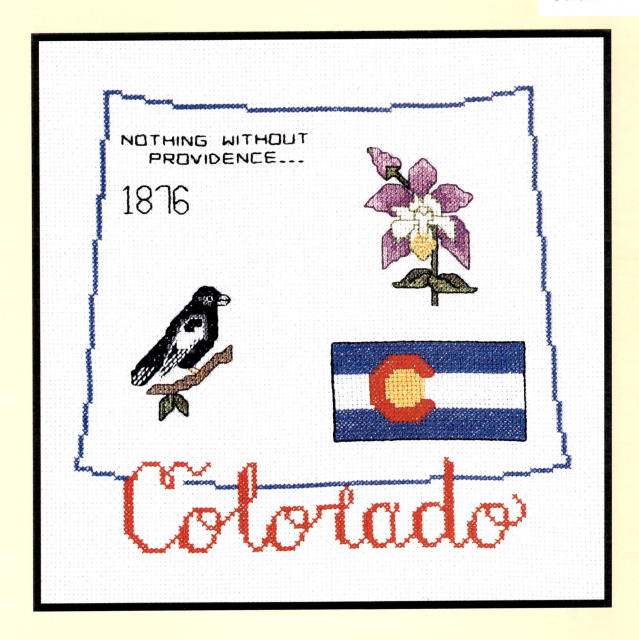

Entered Union: August 1, 1876
38th state
Bird: Lark bunting
Flower: Rocky Mountain columbine
Nickname: Centennial State

If the salient features of any state can be focused in a single letter of the alphabet, the big, bold, red letter "C" in Colorado's flag provides such a focus. Colorado is the Centennial State, having entered the Union one month after the 100th anniversary of the United States. The Rocky Mountain columbine is the state flower. The red of the large "C" that took its present place in the blue and white striped flag only in 1964 tells us that the Spanish word, *colorado,* means ruddy. The present appearance of the flag has evolved during the years from 1911 to 1964.

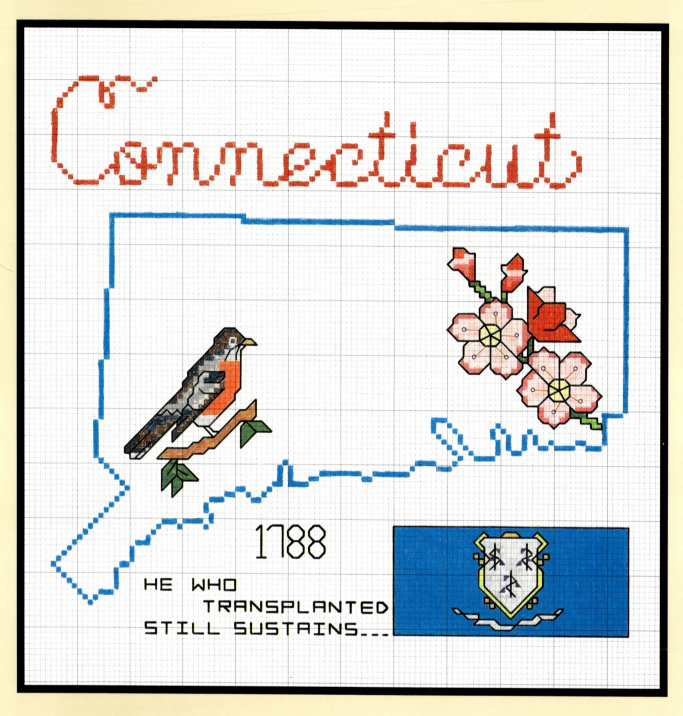

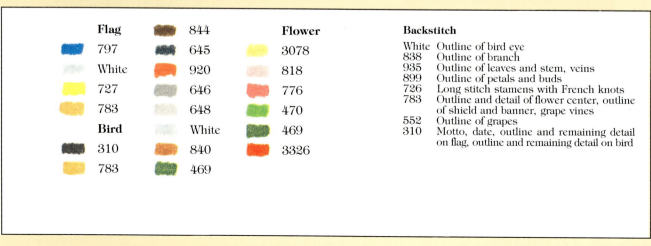

CONNECTICUT

Entered Union:	January 9, 1778
	5th state
Bird:	American robin
Flower:	Mountain laurel
Nicknames:	Nutmeg State
	Constitution State
	Land of Steady Habits

The motto of the state of Connecticut "He Who Transplanted Still Sustains," is a verbal expression of the visual motif of that state's flag. It shows three grapevines—one for each of the state's three earliest settlements: Hartford, Wetherford, and Windsor. Those three outposts, founded by settlers from the Massachusetts Bay Colony, were united under a charter granted by Charles II of England in 1622.

The flag has a white rococco shield, an azure field bordered in yellow and silver, and the three grapevines which, with their green vegetation, emblemize the abundance that the state's earliest settlers first encountered.

The colony of Connecticut produced the first written constitution of colonial North America.

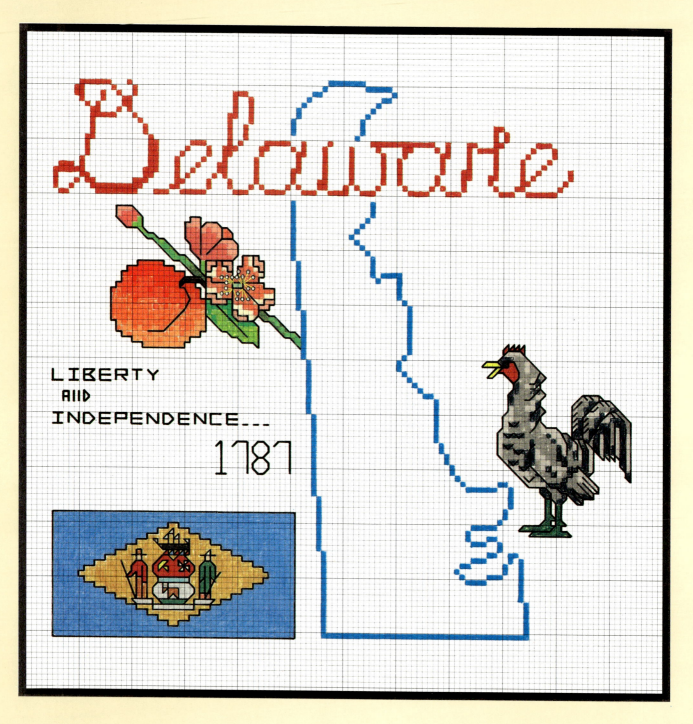

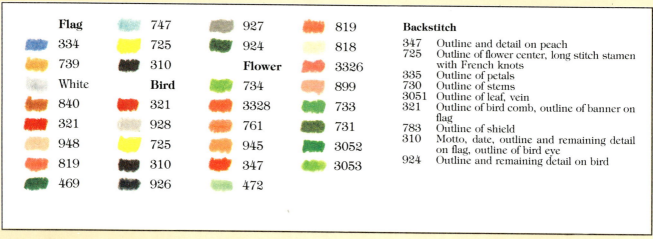

Flag				Backstitch	
334	747	927	819	347	Outline and detail on peach
739	725	924	818	725	Outline of flower center, long stitch stamen with French knots
White	310	**Flower**	3326	335	Outline of petals
840	**Bird**	734	899	730	Outline of stems
321	321	3328	733	3051	Outline of leaf, vein
948	928	761	731	321	Outline of bird comb, outline of banner on flag
819	725	945	3052	783	Outline of shield
469	310	347	3053	310	Motto, date, outline and remaining detail on flag, outline of bird eye
	926	472		924	Outline and remaining detail on bird

DELAWARE

Entered Union:	December 7, 1787
	1st state
Bird:	Blue hen chicken
Flower:	Peach blossom
Nicknames:	First State
	Diamond State
	Peach State

Delaware's contributions to the Union have been great despite her small size. A Delawarian cast the decisive vote that resulted in the adoption of the Declaration of Independence, and Delaware was the first state to ratify the United States Constitution.

   The colors of the Delaware flag, blue and buff, were chosen by General George Washington for the uniforms of his Delaware riflemen. The wheat, corn, and ox on the shield symbolize Sussex, Kent, and Newcastle (the three "lower" counties of William Penn's original grant for the colony of Pennsylvania), which were to become Delaware. A farmer and a rifleman are shown supporting the shield, as they supported, from the very beginning, those notions of liberty and independence that gave birth to these United States.

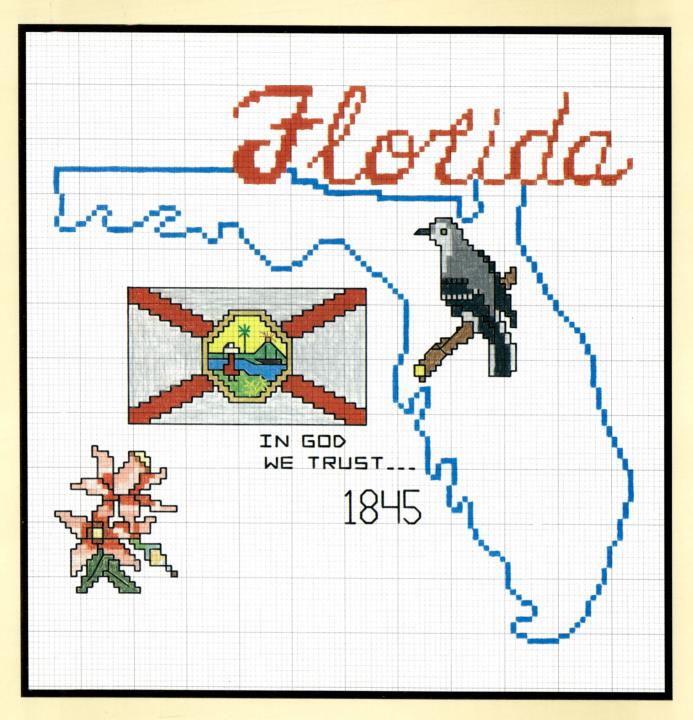

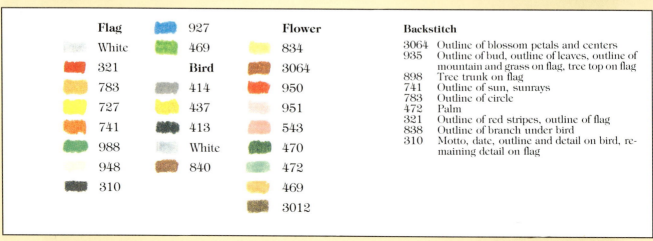

Flag		Flower	Backstitch	
White	927	834	3064	Outline of blossom petals and centers
321	469	3064	935	Outline of bud, outline of leaves, outline of mountain and grass on flag, tree top on flag
783	Bird	950	898	Tree trunk on flag
727	414	951	741	Outline of sun, sunrays
741	437	543	783	Outline of circle
988	413	470	472	Palm
948	White	472	321	Outline of red stripes, outline of flag
310	840	469	838	Outline of branch under bird
		3012	310	Motto, date, outline and detail on bird, remaining detail on flag

FLORIDA

Entered Union:	March 3, 1845
	27th state
Bird:	Mockingbird
Flower:	Orange blossom
Nicknames:	Sunshine State
	Peninsula State
	Everglades State

The original state flag of Florida was adopted in 1868 and showed the state seal on a plain white ground. The centered seal shows a Seminole woman and a palm tree, symbolic elements which are essentially Floridian, as well as a steamboat, a common 19th-century sign of progress. However, over 15,000 Floridians had fought in the Confederate army, and, by the turn of the century, feeling was strong in the state that the plain white ground behind the seal seemed a sign of surrender. For this reason, a red St. Andrew's cross was added to the white ground, commemorating Florida's contribution to the Confederacy.

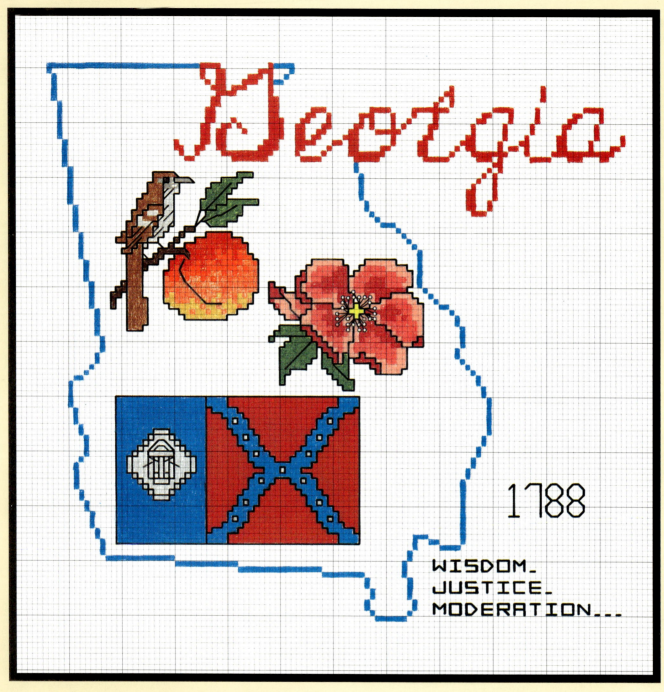

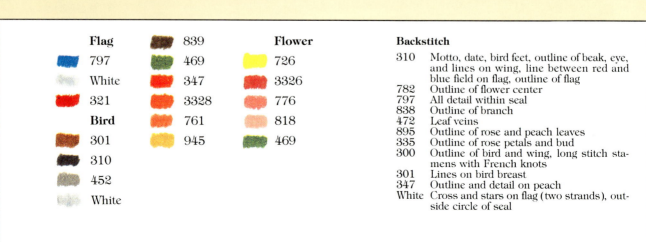

GEORGIA

Entered Union: January 2, 1788
4th state
Bird: Brown thrasher
Flower: Cherokee rose
Nicknames: Peach State
Empire State of the South
Cracker State

Georgia, one of the original 13 colonies, was named for George II of England. Georgia ratified the new U. S. constitution and gained statehood in 1788. Ten years later, a state seal was adopted. It emphasized the importance of the Constitution, using the device of three pillars to represent wisdom, justice, and moderation which support the legislative, judicial, and executive bodies authorized by the Constitution. A Minuteman is shown standing ready to defend the values signified on the seal.

On July 1, 1956 the Georgia legislature authorized a state flag that combined symbols of both the 18th and 19th centuries. The staff third of the flag shows the 1799 seal on a blue field. The two-thirds of the flag at the fly is the Confederate Battle Flag.

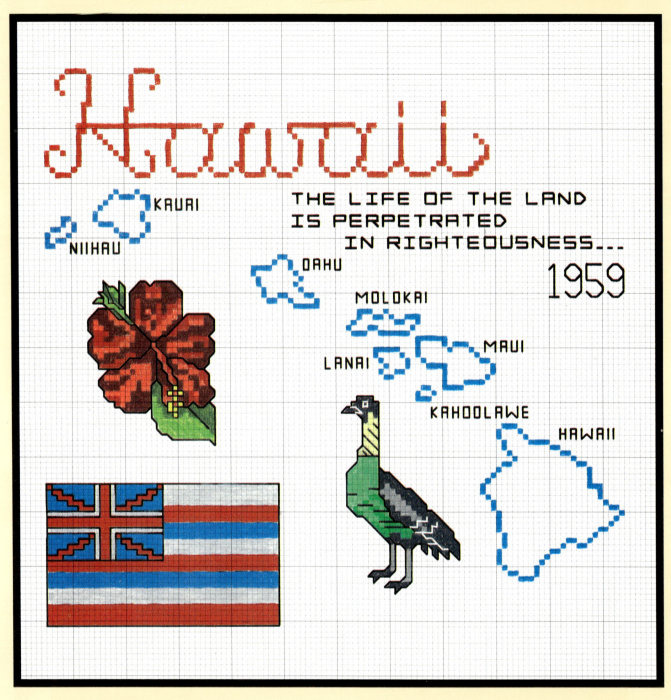

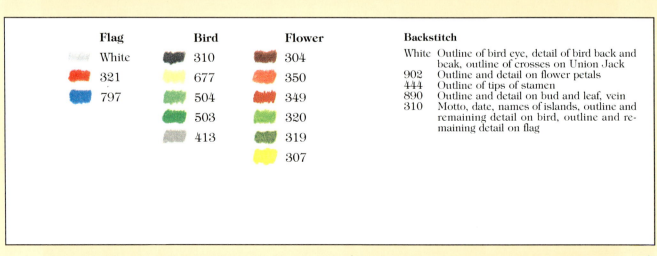

Flag	Bird	Flower	Backstitch	
White	310	304	White	Outline of bird eye, detail of bird back and beak, outline of crosses on Union Jack
321	677	350	902	Outline and detail on flower petals
797	504	349	444	Outline of tips of stamen
	503	320	890	Outline and detail on bud and leaf, vein
	413	319	310	Motto, date, names of islands, outline and remaining detail on bird, outline and remaining detail on flag
		307		

HAWAII

Entered Union: August 21, 1959
50th state
Bird: Nene (Hawaiian goose)
Flower: Hibiscus
Nickname: Aloha State

The state flag of Hawaii is unique in that it is an exact and open tribute to a foreign nation. The state flag of Hawaii, with eight red, white, and blue stripes, incorporates the British Union Jack in its upper staff quadrant, because two famed British explorers played crucial roles in that state's history. Captain James Cooke visited the islands in 1778 and called the group the Sandwich Islands. (In the early 1790s, King Kamehameha I united the islands into a single kingdom, Hawaii.)

In 1793, Captain George Vancouver presented Kamehameha with a Union Jack. In the following year, the king accepted an informal British protectorate, never ratified by the British government. In 1816, the first Hawaiian ship to sail abroad flew the current flag with its eight stripes—one for each of the eight islands in the group: Hawaii, Maui, Oahu, Kauai, Molokai, Lanai, Niihau and Kahoolawe. In 1893, Queen Liliuokalani was deposed, and Hawaii asked for annexation to the United States. Congress voted for annexation in 1898. Hawaii became a territory in 1900 and the 50th state in 1959—with her state flag still displaying the Union Jack.

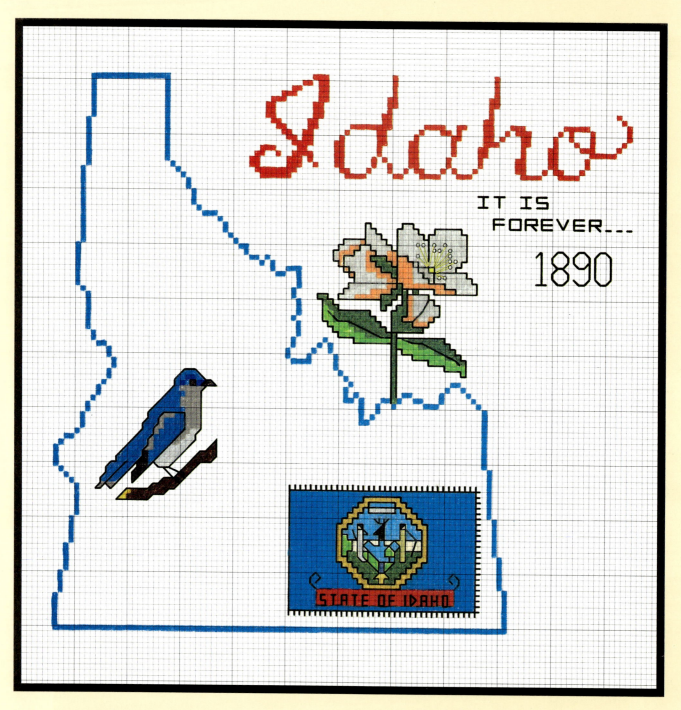

Flag	930	840		**Backstitch**
797	738	437		797 Outline of flag
321	948	800		782 Fringe
782	**Bird**	**Flower**		White Scrolls on bottom banner, "STATE OF IDAHO"
747	518	725		470 Outline of flower petals
White	310	White		725 Outline of flower center, long stitch stamens with French knots
469	930	Ecru		935 Outline of leaves and stem, veins
470	932	469		838 Outline of branch
739	White	470		310 Motto, date, remaining detail on flag, outline of bird beak and eye, feet
				823 Outline and remaining detail on bird

IDAHO

Entered Union:	July 3, 1890
	43rd state
Bird:	Mountain bluebird
Flower:	Syringia
Nicknames:	Gem State
	Spud State
	Panhandle State

The Idaho shield, designed when the state entered the Union in the last decade of the 19th century, has all the marks of its Victorian time. It is jammed with almost every symbol that could be devised. Crested by the head of a buck elk, supported on one side by Liberty with her Phrygian cap and spear, and on the other by Justice with her sword and scales, the shield shows the single white star marking Idaho's entry into the nation, as well as a mining man and a woman on equal footing—a reference to Idaho's early lead in women's suffrage. Depictions of the Snake River, cornucopias, and, of course, potatoes fill the rest of the available space on the shield. The whole is ringed in yellow, with the words, "The Great Seal of Idaho." The flag shows the seal centered on a blue field.

Flag	Bird	Flower	Backstitch	
White	817	553	321	Outline and detail of shield, outline and detail on banner
898	310	554	White	Outline of bird eye
726	921	469	921	Outline of bird beak
797	814	470	310	Motto, date, outline and remaining detail on flag, outline and remaining detail on bird
321	498		838	Outline of branch
434	840		782	Fringe
	437		726	Sunrays, French knot flower centers
			550	Outline of flower petals and buds
			934	Outline of leaves, veins, stems, olive branch on flag

ILLINOIS

Entered Union:	December 3, 1818
	21st state
Bird:	Cardinal
Flower:	Native violet
Nicknames:	Prairie State
	Land of Lincoln
	Tall State
	Sucker State

The name "Illinois" comes from the French *illini*, which means "a tribe of superior men." The image of an American eagle clutching an olive branch with a shield and a golden sunrise became the state seal in 1810, and the design has changed little since then. On the red ribbon in the eagle's claws, the words "State Sovereignty" originally appeared above the words "National Union." In 1868, following the Civil War, the Secretary of State of Illinois asked the legislature to reverse this word order. The legislature refused, but the maker of the seal contrived to make the words "National Union" more legible and appear to be above the words "State Sovereignty," without actually changing the order of the words on the ribbon.

The flag, adopted in its current form in 1970, shows the state seal on a white field.

Flag	Bird	Flower	Backstitch	
797	817	746	White	Outline of bird eye
725	310	White	921	Outline of bird beak
	921	469	310	Motto, date, outline and detail on bird, feet
	498	3364	838	Outline and detail on branch
	814	937	934	Outline of leaves and stem, veins
	840		725	Outline of stars, light beams
	437		782	Outline of flag, long stitch stamens with French knots
			437	Outline of petals
			797	Outline and detail on torch

INDIANA

Entered State: December 11, 1816
19th state
Bird: Cardinal
Flower: Peony
Nickname: Hoosier State

Stars, stars, and more golden stars radiate from a golden torch of liberty and enlightenment on a blue ground on the state flag of Indiana. There are 19 golden stars representing the then 19 states; the largest for Indiana, herself.

As with most state flags that have a blue background, the Indiana's flag has its origin in the regimental color carried by the state's militia. It was adopted in 1917, when the Indiana regiment departed for Europe and World War I.

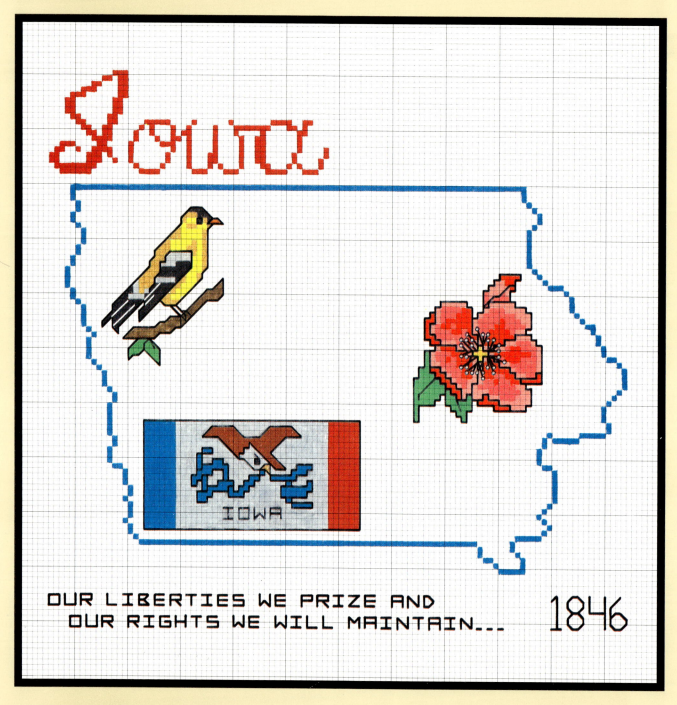

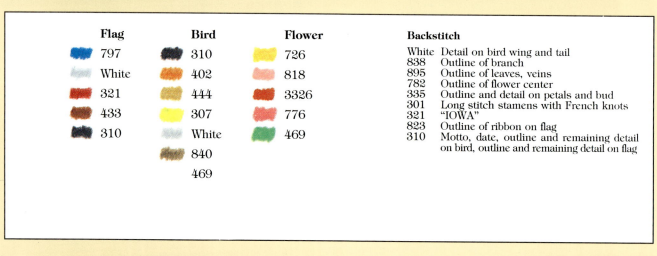

Flag	Bird	Flower	Backstitch	
797	310	726	White	Detail on bird wing and tail
White	402	818	838	Outline of branch
321	444	3326	895	Outline of leaves, veins
433	307	776	782	Outline of flower center
310	White	469	335	Outline and detail on petals and bud
	840		301	Long stitch stamens with French knots
	469		321	"IOWA"
			823	Outline of ribbon on flag
			310	Motto, date, outline and remaining detail on bird, outline and remaining detail on flag

IOWA

Entered Union: December 28, 1846
29th state
Bird: Eastern goldfinch
Flower: Wild rose
Nicknames: Corn State
Hawkeye State
Breadbasket State
The Beautiful Land

Deep in America's heartland, Iowa's first European visitors were French, and the Iowa territory entered the United States as part of the Louisiana Purchase. Although Hawaii flies the only exact replica of a foreign flag, the tricolor of France is given more than passing remembrance on Iowa's flag.

Although Iowa entered the Union in 1846, all attempts to adopt a state flag after 1865 were opposed by the Union veterans of the Grand Army of the Republic (G.A.R.), on the grounds that the Stars and Stripes of the United States were sufficient for any state. In 1921, the Iowa legislature adopted the present state colors. In the white central field, the American bald eagle carries the words of the state motto. It is still referred to as a banner, not a flag, in memory of the strong feelings of the Iowa G.A.R.

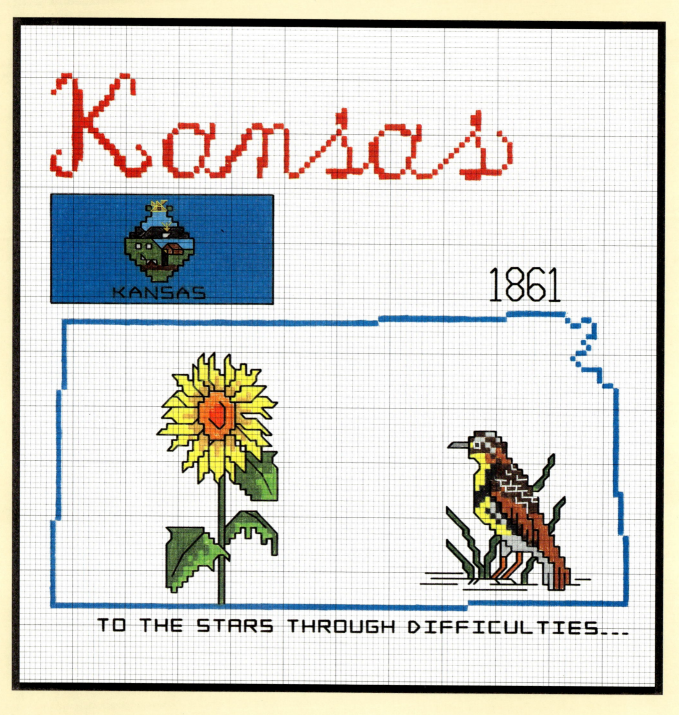

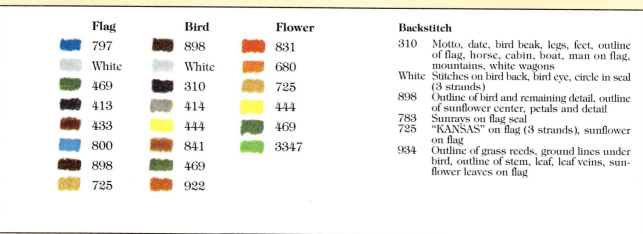

Flag	Bird	Flower	Backstitch	
797	898	831	310	Motto, date, bird beak, legs, feet, outline of flag, horse, cabin, boat, man on flag, mountains, white wagons
White	White	680	White	Stitches on bird back, bird eye, circle in seal (3 strands)
469	310	725	898	Outline of bird and remaining detail, outline of sunflower center, petals and detail
413	414	444	783	Sunrays on flag seal
433	444	469	725	"KANSAS" on flag (3 strands), sunflower on flag
800	841	3347	934	Outline of grass reeds, ground lines under bird, outline of stem, leaf, leaf veins, sunflower leaves on flag
898	469			
725	922			

KANSAS

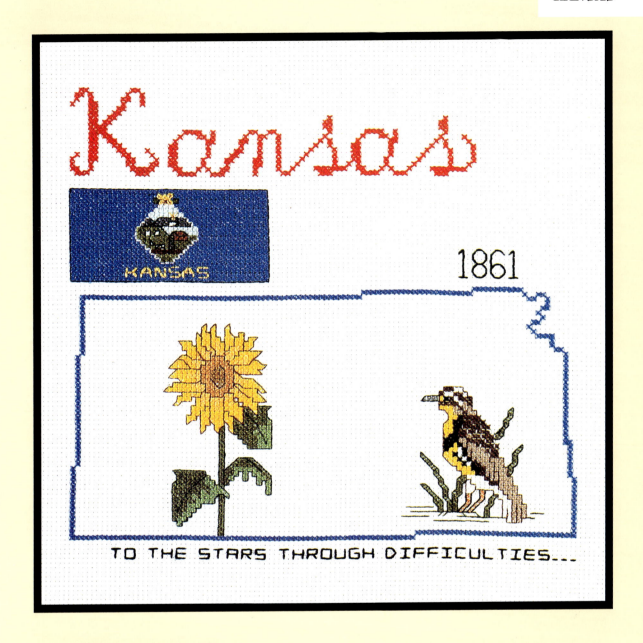

Entered Union:	January 29, 1861
	34th state
Bird:	Western meadowlark
Flower:	Sunflower
Nicknames:	Sunflower State
	Jayhawk State

Kansas entered the Union as the 34th state during the first year of the Civil War. There was considerable dissension at the time as to whether Kansas should enter as a "slave" or "free" state. Kansas adopted the motto, *Ad Aspera Per Astra* (Through Difficulty to the Stars). The rather crowded Victorian state shield is crowned by the image of a sunflower emerging from a heraldic wreath of twisting blue and gold. The interior of the shield shows a veritable "Home on the Range"—rolling hills beyond a prairie, with a settler's cabin, a farmer, a bison, a covered wagon moving westward, a band of Indians—and even that popular 19th-century harbinger of progress, the steamboat.

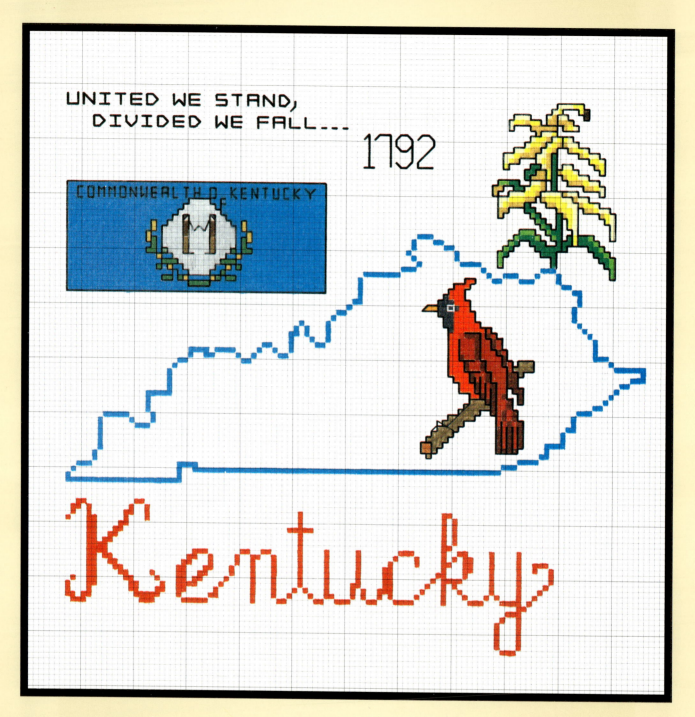

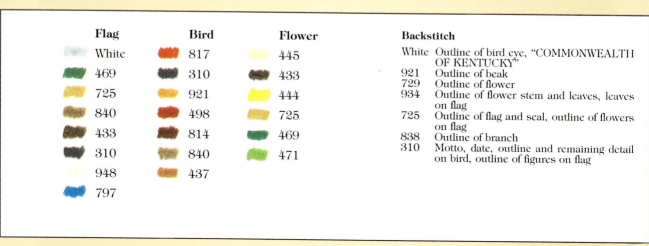

Flag		Bird		Flower		Backstitch	
	White		817		445	White	Outline of bird eye, "COMMONWEALTH OF KENTUCKY"
	469		310		433	921	Outline of beak
	725		921		444	729	Outline of flower
	840		498		725	934	Outline of flower stem and leaves, leaves on flag
	433		814		469	725	Outline of flag and seal, outline of flowers on flag
	310		840		471	838	Outline of branch
	948		437			310	Motto, date, outline and remaining detail on bird, outline of figures on flag
	797						

KENTUCKY

Entered Union: June 1, 1792
15th state
Bird: Cardinal
Flower: Goldenrod
Nickname: Bluegrass State

Kentucky, the first "Western" state to enter the Union, took her motto from the refrain of a popular song of the American Revolution. That motto—"United We Stand, Divided We Fall"—came to have increased meaning when Kentucky, a border state, opted to stay within the Union during the Civil War.

    The state seal, centered on the blue field of the state flag, shows a buckskin-clad frontiersman clasping hands and arms with an elegant gentleman in city dress—the new wilderness joining with the old former colonies of the East in what would become a lasting bond. The picture of the green-sprigged goldenrod, Kentucky's state flower, surrounds the shield. The image of the state bird, the cardinal, surmounts the flagstaff when formally displayed.

Flag	318	**Flower**	**Backstitch**
797	830	3047	White — Detail on wing
725	898	676	937 — Outline of leaves and reeds
White	842	3024	725 — Chick beaks
310	747	White	782 — Outline of nest, outline of stamen, fringe
Bird	807	937	830 — Outline of petals
842	3348	471	310 — Motto, date, outline and remaining detail on bird, outline and remaining detail on flag
762	3347		

LOUISIANA

Entered State:	April 30, 1812
	18th state
Bird:	Brown pelican
Flower:	Magnolia
Nicknames:	Bayou State
	Pelican State
	Creole State
	Sugar State

References to a pelican's image on the flag flying over Louisiana go back to the early 19th century. In 1862, Admiral Farragut removed just such a "pelican" flag from the Louisiana statehouse when he captured Baton Rouge from the Confederacy.

The present flag was adopted in 1912, but not until 1966 did the brown pelican become the official state bird. The pelican shown on the state flag, with her three hungry chicks, differs from the one shown on the more detailed state seal in that, in the seal, the mother pelican has pierced her own breast with her beak to feed her young with her own blood. This ancient symbol, widely used in heraldry, is derived from the myth that the European pelican got its red-tipped beak in this self-sacrificing fashion.

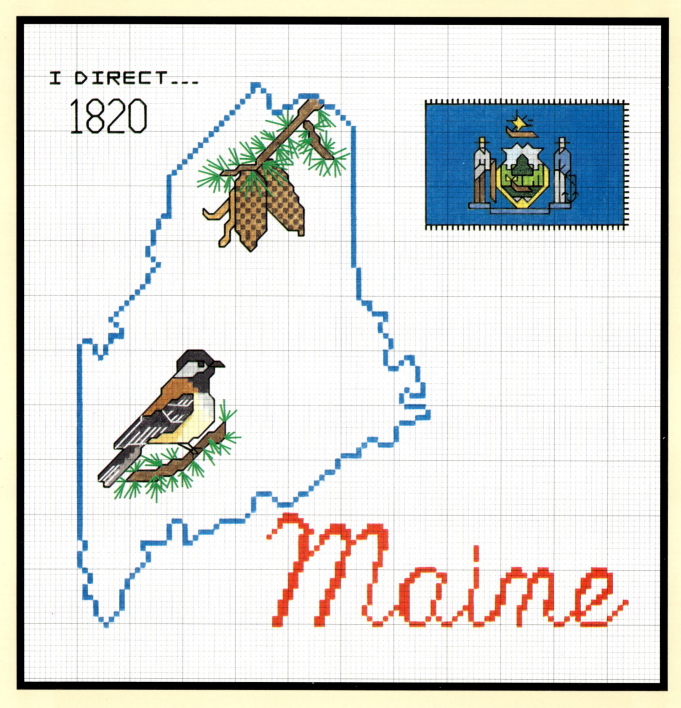
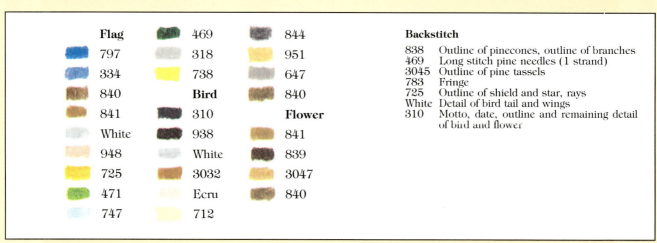

			Backstitch	
Flag	469	844	838	Outline of pinecones, outline of branches
797	318	951	469	Long stitch pine needles (1 strand)
334	738	647	3045	Outline of pine tassels
840	**Bird**	840	783	Fringe
841	310	**Flower**	725	Outline of shield and star, rays
White	938	841	White	Detail of bird tail and wings
948	White	839	310	Motto, date, outline and remaining detail of bird and flower
725	3032	3047		
471	Ecru	840		
747	712			

MAINE

Entered Union: March 15, 1820
23rd state
Bird: Chickadee
Flower: White pinecone and tassel
Nickname: Pine Tree State

The white pine, which often grows to a height of 200 feet, was used for the ships' masts that were Maine's most important source of income in the 18th and 19th centuries. A part of Massachusetts until 1820, Maine entered the Union in that year as the northernmost state; hence the motto, *Dirigo* (I Direct), refers to the North Star shown uppermost on the blue state flag. A bull moose is pictured resting placidly beneath the tall pine on the state seal, which is flanked by a farmer with his scythe and a beribboned sailor in white and blue. Maine derives her name from the French province, Mayne, which was ruled by Henrietta Maria, the wife of Charles I of England.

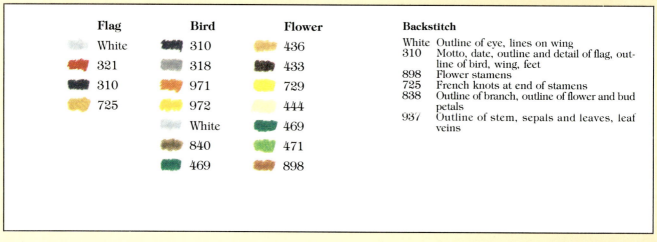

Flag	Bird	Flower	Backstitch	
White	310	436	White	Outline of eye, lines on wing
321	318	433	310	Motto, date, outline and detail of flag, outline of bird, wing, feet
310	971	729	898	Flower stamens
725	972	444	725	French knots at end of stamens
	White	469	838	Outline of branch, outline of flower and bud petals
	840	471	937	Outline of stem, sepals and leaves, leaf veins
	469	898		

MARYLAND

Entered Union:	April 28, 1788 7th state
State Bird:	Baltimore oriole
State Flower:	Black-eyed Susan
Nicknames:	Old Line State Free State

The state flag of Maryland is unique among state flags—it is pure Old World heraldry. Its history begins in 1629, when Sir George Calvert, the first Lord Baltimore, visited the territory that is now called Maryland (named for Henrietta Maria, wife of Charles I of England). In 1632, Sir George was made Lord Protector of that large American territory. That year his son, Cecilus, second Lord Baltimore, led an expedition to Maryland and brought with him a flag with the Calvert arms quartered with those of his mother's family, the Crosslands of Yorkshire. Thus it is that the bold yellow and black bars of the Calvert family arms (hues echoed by both the black-eyed Susan and the Baltimore oriole) are to this day quartered with the striking scarlet and white crosses of the house of Crossland. The present flag, adopted in 1904, replaced several earlier versions.

Maryland is called the Free State because the Lord Proprietor could make laws only with the consent of the free men of Maryland, and the Old Line State because, in 1732, the surveyors, Mason and Dixon, defined their line as the northern boundary of the state of Maryland.

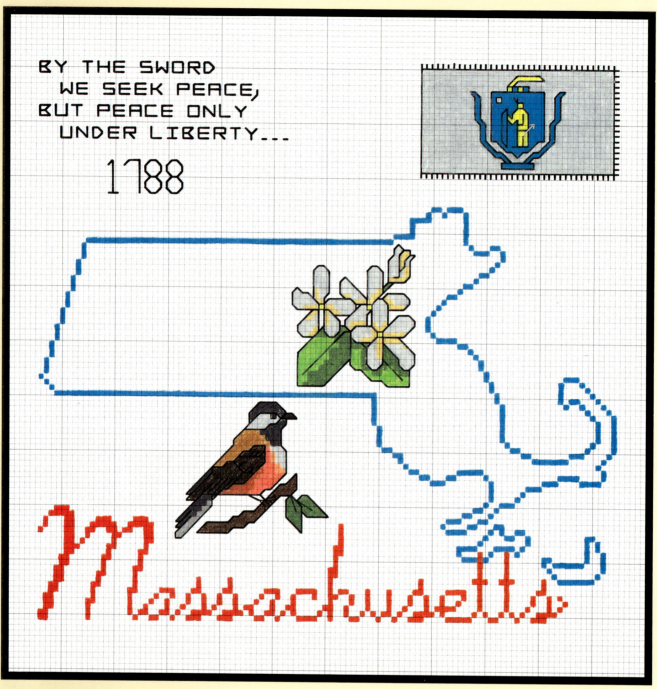

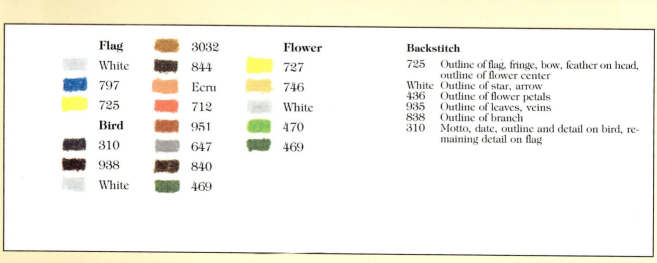

MASSACHUSETTS

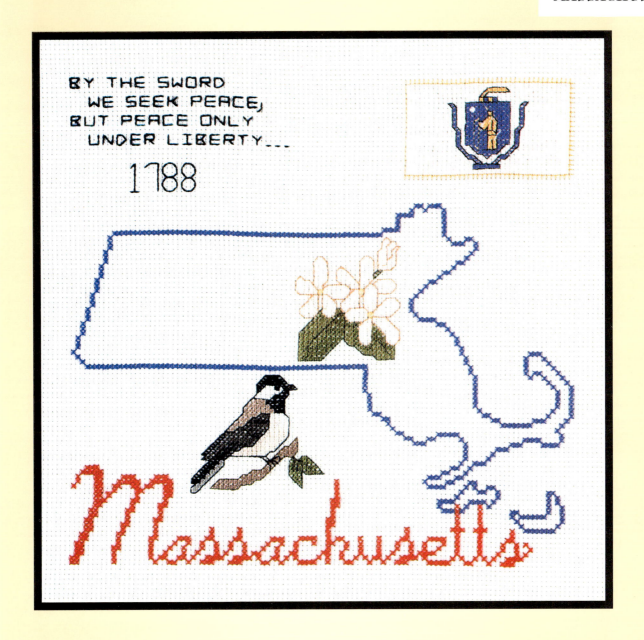

Entered Union: February 6, 1788
 6th state
Bird: Chickadee
Flower: Mayflower
Nickname: Bay State
 Old Bay State
 Old Colony State
 Puritan State
 Baked Bean State

The Wampanoag Indian, Massasoit, exemplified the friendliness of the native Americans who greeted the earliest of Massachusetts settlers at Plymouth. He is honored on the state seal by the image of a magnificent brave with feathers, moccasins and bow. He is shown centered in the seal holding a single arrow at his side that points downward. The background of the shield is blue, and contains a single white star.

Massachusetts's white state flag shows the centered shield and, above it, the crest of a blue and gold wreath. From the wreath issues a right arm, in ruffled colonial sleeve, grasping a sword that also points downward. This symbolizes the state motto, "By the Sword We Seek Peace, but Peace Only under Liberty."

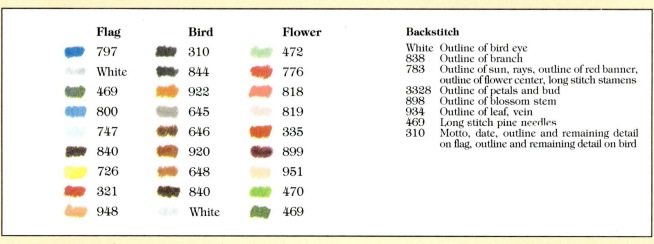

MICHIGAN

Entered Union:	January 26, 1837
	26th state
Bird:	Robin
Flower:	Apple blossom
Nicknames:	Wolverine State
	Water Wonderland

Michigan is a border state and, although our border with Canada is peaceful today, Canada was still very much a British colony when Michigan entered the Union a mere sixty years after the War of Independence. In 1837, Michigan's strategic location on the border of British Canada led to the adoption of a state seal that portrays vigilance with almost all of its symbols. On the state seal centered on the blue-fielded military flag, a man in buckskins is seen standing at the promontory of a peninsula. He is shown looking out over sunlit waters and raising his right arm in the oath, *Tuebor* (I Will Protect). The figure holds a musket in his left hand. The crest is a modification of the U.S. coat of arms, on which is shown an American eagle and the motto, *E Pluribus Unum,* on a red banner. The state motto for this state with many peninsulas is "If You Seek a Pleasant Peninsula, Look about You."

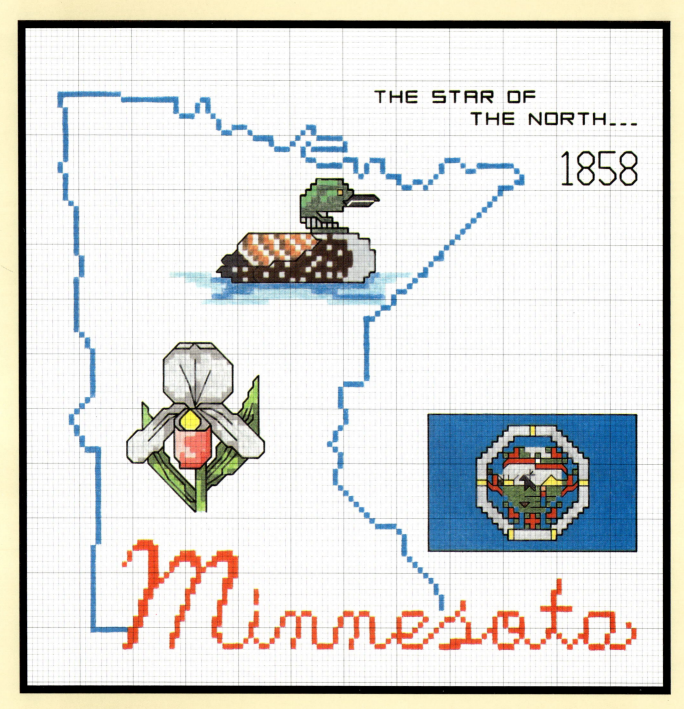

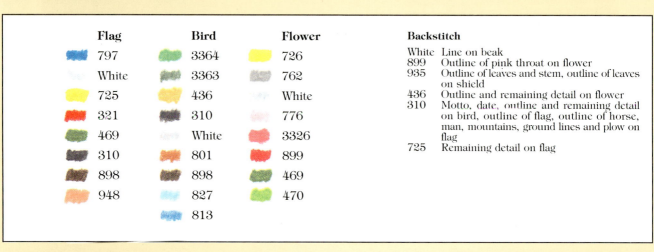

Flag	Bird	Flower	Backstitch	
797	3364	726	White	Line on beak
White	3363	762	899	Outline of pink throat on flower
725	436	White	935	Outline of leaves and stem, outline of leaves on shield
321	310	776	436	Outline and remaining detail on flower
469	White	3326	310	Motto, date, outline and remaining detail on bird, outline of flag, outline of horse, man, mountains, ground lines and plow on flag
310	801	899		
898	898	469		
948	827	470	725	Remaining detail on flag
	813			

MINNESOTA

Entered Union:	May 11, 1858
	32nd state
Bird:	Common loon
Flower:	Pink and white lady's slipper
Nicknames:	North Star State
	Gopher State
	Land of 10,000 Lakes
	Land of Sky Blue Waters

In 1858, Minnesota became the second northernmost state, after Maine, to enter the Union, hence *L' Etoile du Nord* is written on her state seal. Five groups of stars, 19 in all, form the tips of a large five-pointed star that represents Minnesota. The largest of the 19, in the top arm of the large star, represents the North Star. Three dates are shown within a wreath of blossoming pink and white lady's slippers: 1819, the year of the first white settlement; 1858, the year of statehood; and 1893, the year of the adoption of the flag. On the flag are shown the banks of the Mississippi river at St. Anthony's Falls, and a farmer plowing, with musket and powderhorn at the ready, as an Indian brave rides off into the setting sun.

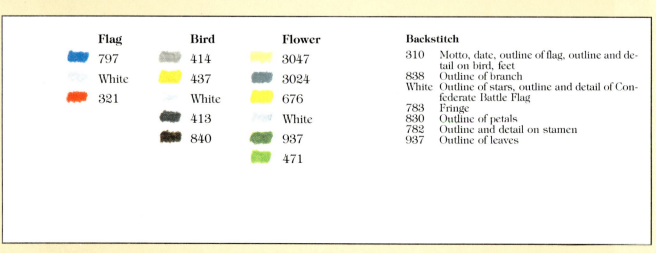

Flag	Bird	Flower	Backstitch	
797	414	3047	310	Motto, date, outline of flag, outline and detail on bird, feet
White	437	3024	838	Outline of branch
321	White	676	White	Outline of stars, outline and detail of Confederate Battle Flag
	413	White	783	Fringe
	840	937	830	Outline of petals
		471	782	Outline and detail on stamen
			937	Outline of leaves

MISSISSIPPI

Entered Union:	December 10, 1817
	20th state
Bird:	Mockingbird
Flower:	Magnolia
Nicknames:	Magnolia State
	Hospitality State

In remembrance of the *Virtue et Arms* motto demonstrated at the Battle of Vicksburg, the state flag of Mississippi proudly flies not one, but very nearly two flags of the Confederacy. The familiar Confederate Battle Flag is at the upper staff quadrant, and the three equally broad red, white, and blue bars, forming the field of the flag, are the exact dimensions of the bars of the Confederate Stars and Bars, although the Battle Flag never had a blue bar.

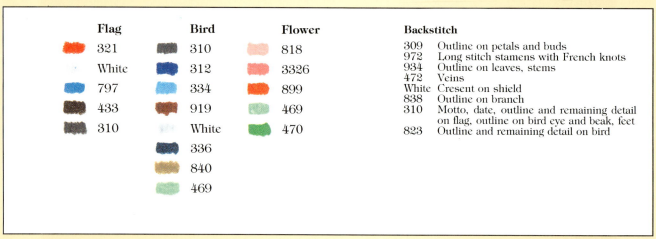

MISSOURI

Entered Union: August 10, 1821
 24th state
Bird: Bluebird
Flower: Hawthorn
Nickname: Show-Me State

On the Missouri state flag, the equal red, white, and blue bands of the tricolor of France appear horizontally in memory of Missouri's addition to the United States as part of the Louisiana Purchase. Within a circular band of blue containing 24 white five-pointed stars is the state seal, whose shield is divided into red, white, and blue segments, containing, respectively, a bear, an American eagle, and a white crescent (another heraldic symbol of the second son) to commemorate Missouri's being the second state formed from the Louisiana Purchase. The shield is supported by two grizzly bears; it is crested by yet another American eagle and surrounded by the state motto. Under the shield are the Roman numerals, MDCCCXX (1820), the year of the Missouri Compromise, when Maine entered the Union as a "free" state and Missouri was designated a "slave" state.

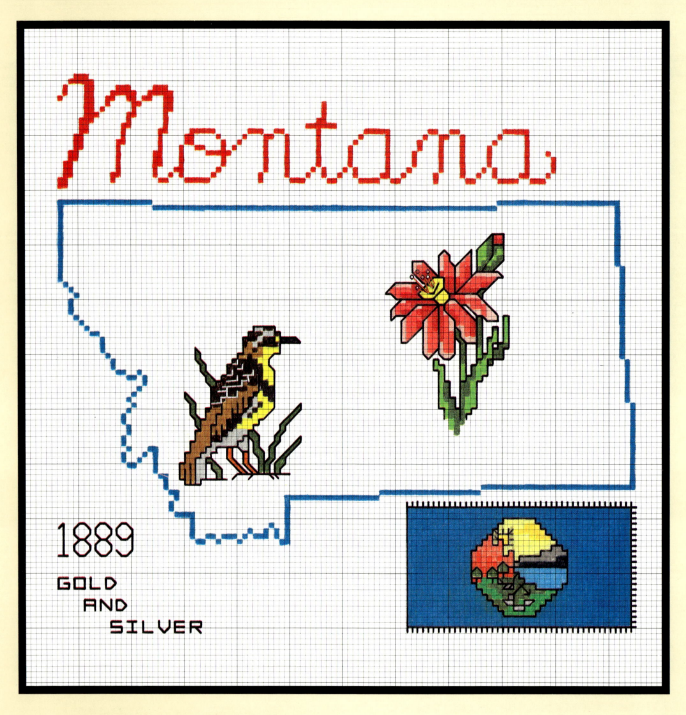

Flag			Backstitch	
797	725	469	309	Outline of flower petals
937	3078	922	783	Outline of flag, fringe, outline of sun, sun-rays, circle on flag, outline of flower center, long stitch stamens with French knots
White	**Bird**	**Flower**		
469	White	726	937	Trunks of trees on flag, outline of flower leaves
747	898	3328	934	Ground lines under bird, outline of reeds
414	310	760	310	Motto, date, outline of bird beak, feet, remaining detail on flag
318	414	761	898	Outline and remaining detail on bird
899	444	469		
818	841	470		

MONTANA

Entered Union:	November 8, 1889
	41st state
Bird:	Western meadowlark
Flower:	Bitterroot
Nickname:	Treasure State

Oro y Plata (silver and gold) is the legend prominently featured in the state seal centered on the blue flag of the Treasure State. The Montana vista shown within the seal is represented by a golden morning sky above silver mountains, and gold, brown, and beige rocks, as well as the great waterfall of the Missouri River. Shown in this tableau are a miner's pick and shovel and a farmer's plow. There is no official indication of the colors to be used in the seal.

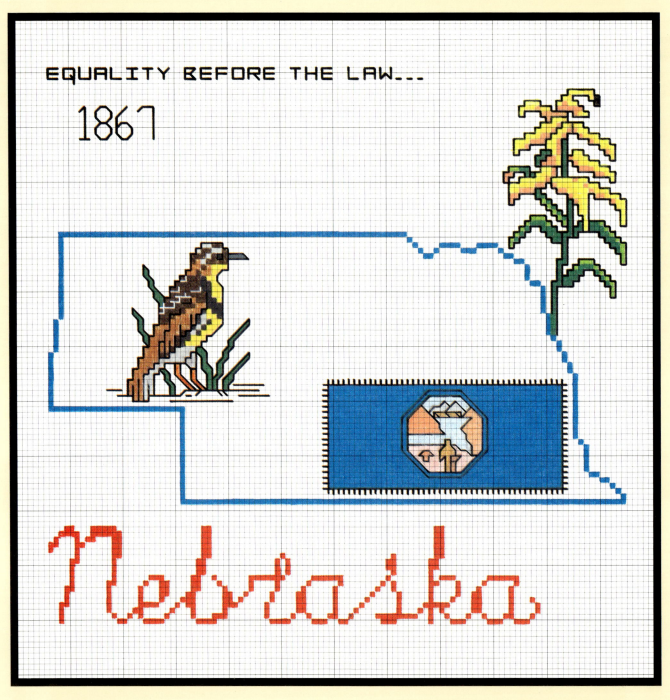
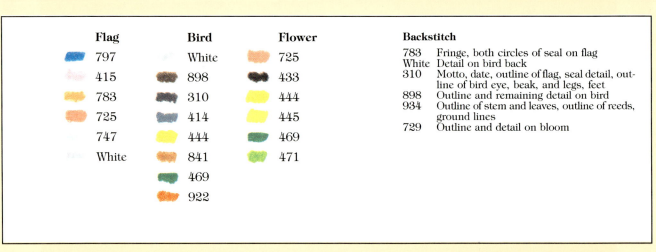

NEBRASKA

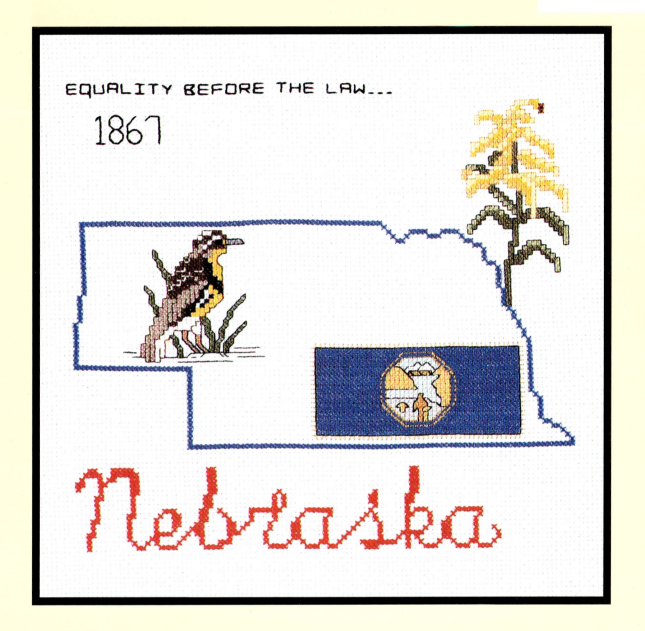

Entered Union: March 1, 1867
37th state
Bird: Western meadowlark
Flower: Goldenrod
Nicknames: Cornhusker State
Beef State
Tree Planters' State

The state flag of Nebraska, adopted in 1925, has a Victorian state seal, predominantly colored in gold and silver; its center shows a golden smith at a golden anvil. Golden sheaves of wheat and stalks of golden corn appear beside a settler's cabin. Also shown are a train heading into the Rockies, which are silver, and a steamboat traveling up the Missouri River.

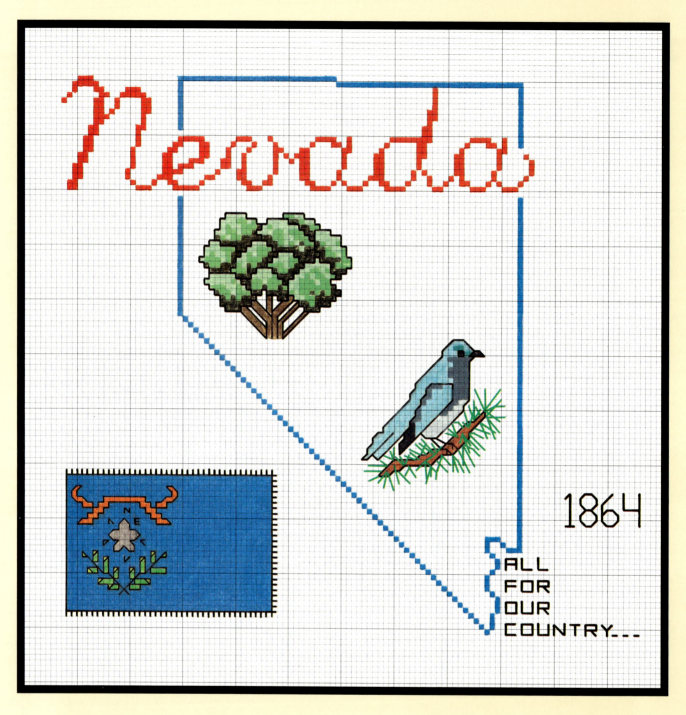

Flag	Bird	Flower	Backstitch	
797	518	841	White	Outline of star
471	310	3051	783	Outline of flag, fringe, outline of banner
727	932	3052	444	Detail around star
783	White	3053	471	Outline of leaves on flag, pine needles (2 strands)
762	433		469	Stems on flag
	930		898	Outline of branches
			936	Outline and remaining detail on sagebrush
			310	Motto, date, outline of bird eye and beak, feet
			823	Outline and remaining detail on bird

NEVADA

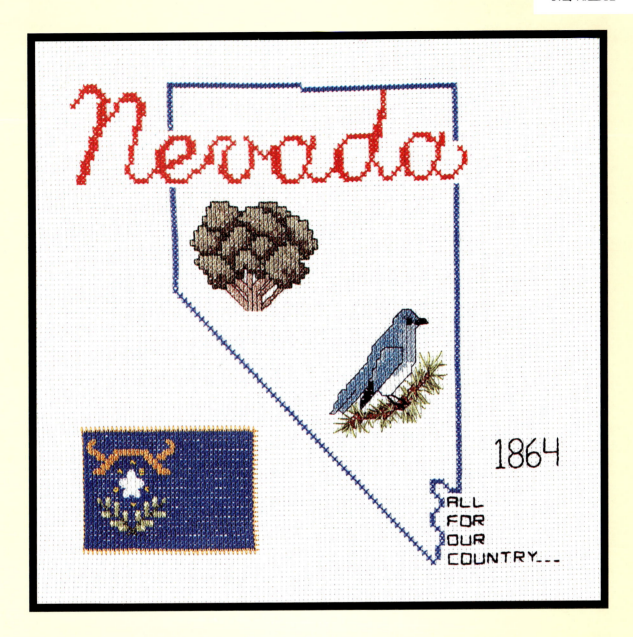

Entered Union:	October 31, 1864
	36th state
Bird:	Mountain bluebird
Flower:	Sagebrush
Nicknames:	Sagebrush State
	Silver State
	Battle Born State

Simple and elegant, the state flag of Nevada, adopted after that state had been part of the Union for almost 60 years, won its designer a $25 prize. Shown on a field of gunmetal blue, a wreath of silver-blue sagebrush surrounds a silver star and upholds the motto, "Battle Born," in the upper staff quadrant.

In 1859, the rich Comstock Lode of silver was discovered. By the middle years of Civil War, the United States government was sufficiently concerned about its gold and silver reserves to welcome Nevada into the Union as the 36th state. Each of the elements in Nevada's flag combine to tell the story of her birth.

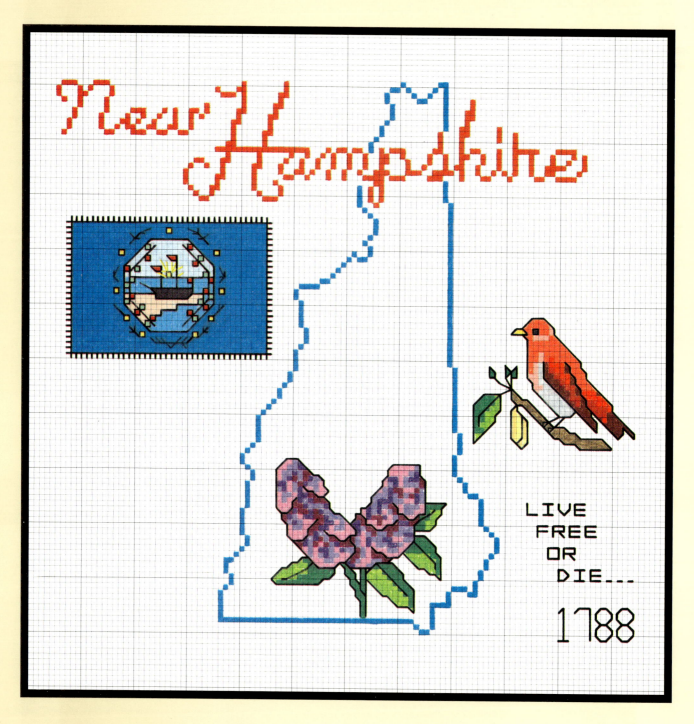

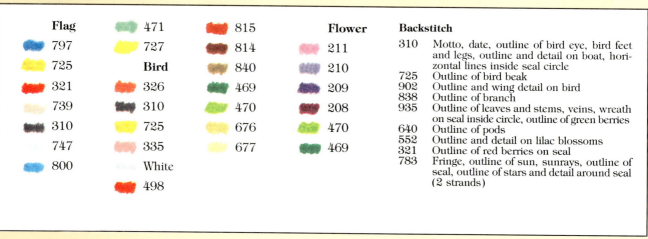

NEW HAMPSHIRE

Entered Union: June 21, 1788
9th state
Bird: Purple finch
Flower: Purple lilac
Nickname: Granite State

The state seal of New Hampshire, shown within a golden laurel wreath interspersed with nine golden stars, centered on a blue field in the state's flag, is historically unique. It bears the first Stars and Stripes as authorized by the Continental Congress on June 14, 1777. The frigate *Raleigh* stands in drydock, rudderless. She was built at Portsmouth and was the first warship to carry the new flag to sea.

The state motto, "Live Free or Die," was first uttered as a toast by General Stark. It was he who in 1777 led the New Hampshire militia against the British, both in the Battle of Bunker Hill and the Battle of Bennington. At Bennington, in what is now Vermont, the militia carried the first Stars and Stripes ever to wave in battle.

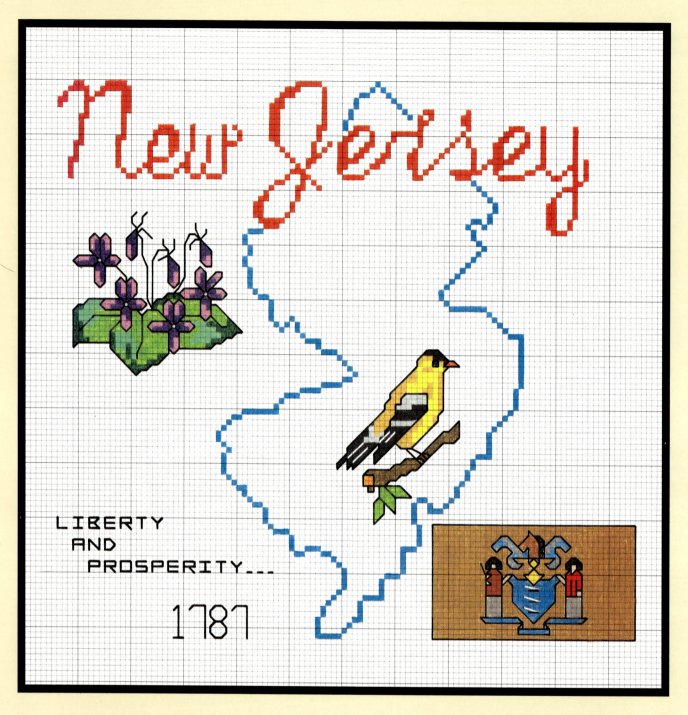

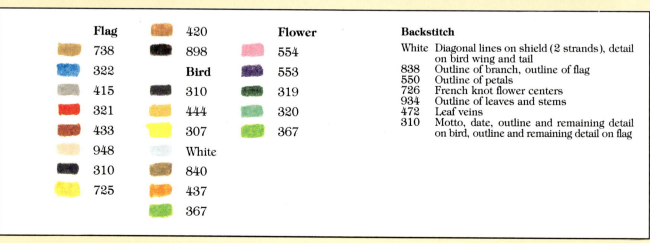

NEW JERSEY

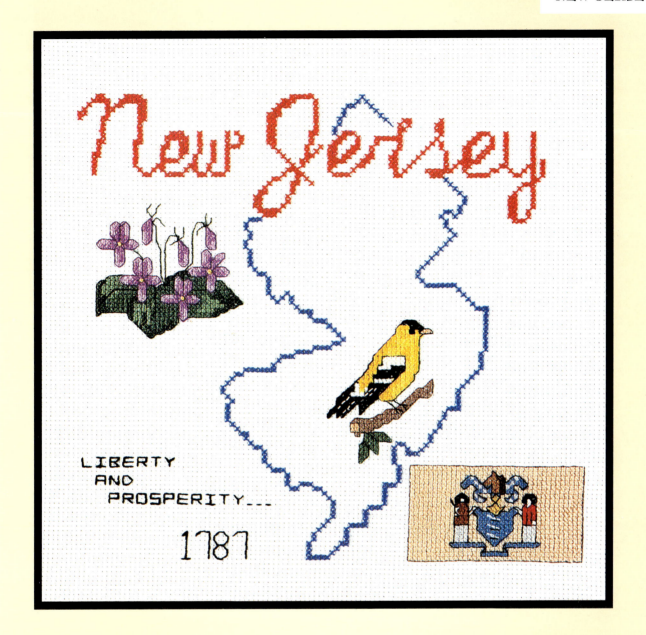

Entered Union:	December 18, 1787
	3rd state
Bird:	Eastern goldfinch
Flower:	Purple violet
Nickname:	The Garden State

The buff background of the state flag of New Jersey is derived from the uniform facings of the New Jersey militia, when they fought with George Washington against the British in 1779. The state seal, which forms the centerpiece of the flag, was created by Pierre Eugene du Simitiere, the designer of the Great Seal of the United States.

The state seal is crested by the image of a horse's head mantled in silver and blue. This rests on a knight's helmet (the heraldic symbol of sovereignty). The helmet rests in turn on a blue shield showing three plows. The shield is supported on one side by Ceres, with her cornucopia (symbol of plentifulness), and on the other by Liberty, with her Phrygian cap. The ancient Phrygians gave such a cap, as a sign of freedom, to those slaves that they liberated.

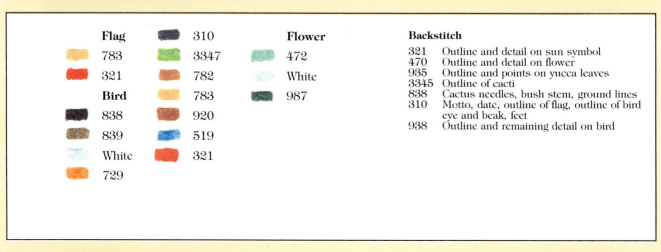

NEW MEXICO

Entered Union:	January 6, 1912
	47th state
Bird:	Roadrunner
Flower:	Yucca
Nicknames:	Land of Enchantment
	Sunshine State

The maxim, "less is more," was never more strikingly in evidence than in the elegant symbolism of the state flag of New Mexico. The ancient red sun symbol of the Zia Pueblo Indians, among the earliest of New Mexico's inhabitants, is powerful and solitary on a field of gold. The colors of the flag echo the gold and red banner of Queen Isabella of Spain, which was carried to the territory by Coronado in the 16th century. The Zia sun is a symbol of perfect friendship among cultures and was used as the floor plan of the New Mexico State capitol.

    The flag was designed by a Dr. Harry Mera, a New Mexican physician-archeologist, and was adopted in 1925.

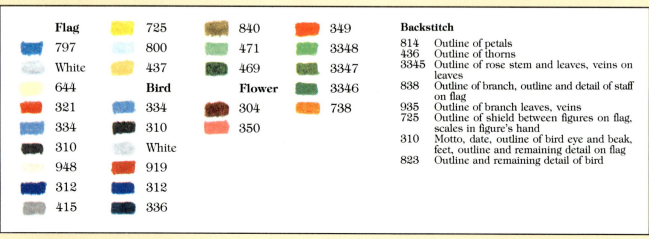

NEW YORK

Entered Union: July 26, 1788
11th state
Bird: Bluebird
Flower: Rose
Nickname: The Empire State

In 1779, the 3rd New York Regiment carried a flag bearing the state arms, on a buff ground, into Yorktown. In 1882, those arms were modified into a state seal and applied to the center of the first state flag. In 1907, the background color of the flag was changed from buff to blue. The seal is crested by a globe showing the New World surmounted by an eagle. On the left it is supported by the tall figure of Liberty, brushing aside a fallen crown at her feet. On the right of the shield stands Justice with her sword and scales. In the shield itself, a sun (the ancient badge of the Dukes of York, who were given control of the colony in 1664) rises over both a ship and a sloop, demonstrating progressive activity on the Hudson River. A white scroll at the base of the shield bears the state motto, *Excelsior* (Ever Upward).

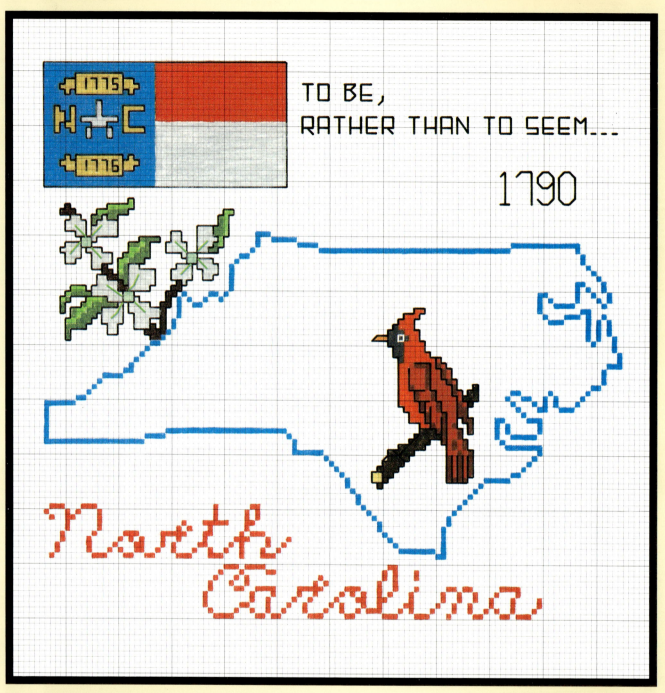

OREGON

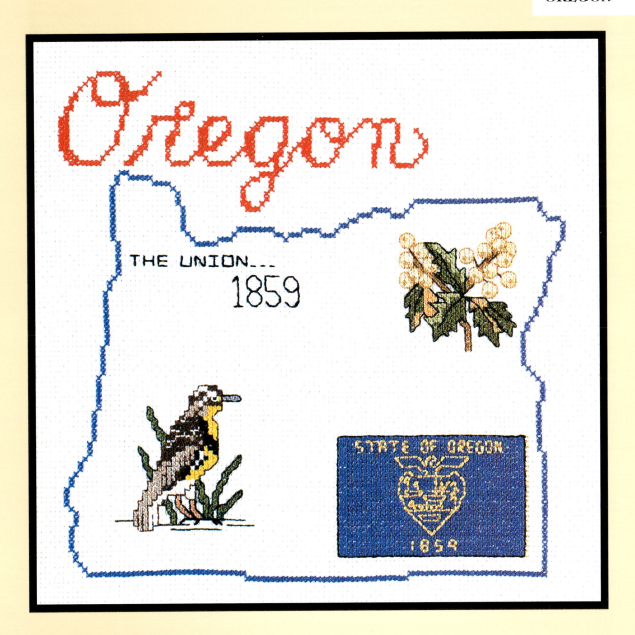

Entered Union: February 14, 1859
33rd state
Bird: Western meadowlark
Flower: Oregon grape
Nickname: The Beaver State

Oregon now has the only remaining state flag with a different design on its reverse side. One side carries the state seal, all in gold, on a blue field. The reverse side shows a golden beaver also on a blue field. The state seal is heart-shaped, indicating Oregon's Valentine's Day entry into the Union, and it is crested by an American eagle with its wings spread. Pictured under a setting sun over the Pacific, an American steamship arrives, as a British man-of-war departs. Also pictured are an elk, fir trees, mountains, a plow and sheaf, a miner's pickaxe, and a covered wagon, which has reached the end of the Oregon Trail. The words "The Union" appear at the bottom of the seal that is outlined on its lower borders. The name "OREGON" appears above and the date "1859" below.

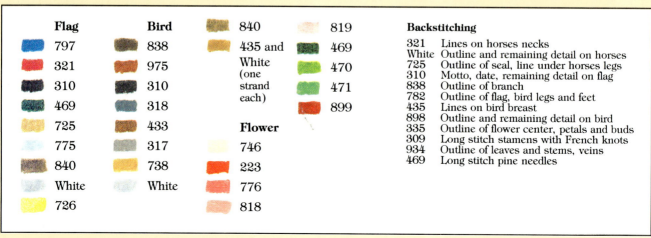

Flag	Bird			Backstitching	
797	838	840	819	321	Lines on horses necks
321	975	435 and White (one strand each)	469	White	Outline and remaining detail on horses
310	310		470	725	Outline of seal, line under horses legs
469	318		471	310	Motto, date, remaining detail on flag
725	433		899	838	Outline of branch
775	317	Flower		782	Outline of flag, bird legs and feet
840	738	746		435	Lines on bird breast
White	White	223		898	Outline and remaining detail on bird
726		776		335	Outline of flower center, petals and buds
		818		309	Long stitch stamens with French knots
				934	Outline of leaves and stems, veins
				469	Long stitch pine needles

PENNSYLVANIA

Entered Union:	December 12, 1787
	2nd state
Bird:	Ruffled grouse
Flower:	Mountain laurel
Nicknames:	Keystone State,
	Quaker State

Pennsylvania was first seen by Europeans in 1609, when Henry Hudson sailed up the Delaware River, but it was not settled by Europeans until the Swedish settled at Chester in 1643.

Pennsylvania's flag shows the state seal centered on a blue field. It is supported by two huge black horses, which symbolize the historical stability of the Keystone State since the time of William Penn. The shield rests on an ornate gold base, and at its crest is an American eagle ready to fly.

The shield is divided into three panels: pictured at the top is a colonial sailing ship; in the center, a plow; in the bottom panel are three sheaves of wheat. Below the shield, an olive branch and a cornstalk are crossed and, on the gold base, a red scroll carries the state motto, "Virtue, Liberty, and Independence," in black letters.

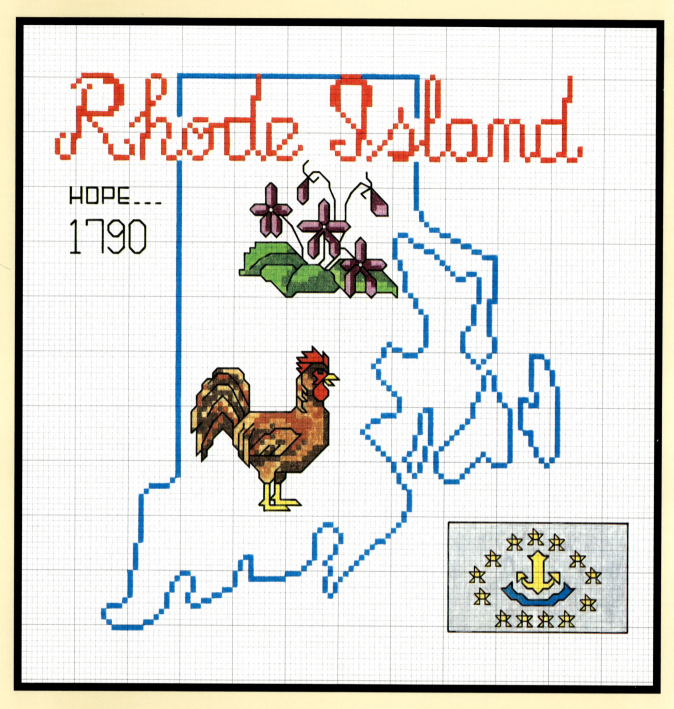

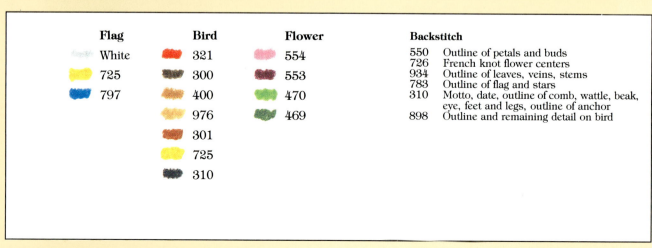

Flag	Bird	Flower	Backstitch	
White	321	554	550	Outline of petals and buds
725	300	553	726	French knot flower centers
797	400	470	934	Outline of leaves, veins, stems
	976	469	783	Outline of flag and stars
	301		310	Motto, date, outline of comb, wattle, beak, eye, feet and legs, outline of anchor
	725		898	Outline and remaining detail on bird
	310			

RHODE ISLAND

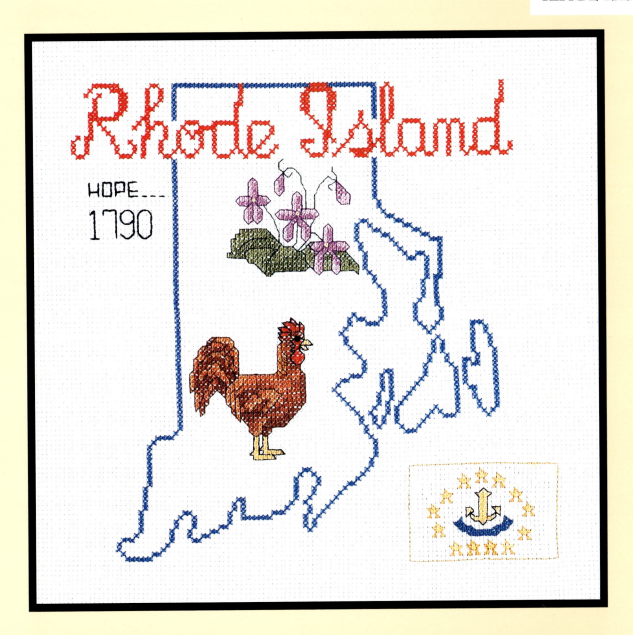

Entered Union:	May 29, 1790
	13th state
Bird:	Rhode Island red chicken
Flower:	Violet
Nicknames:	Little Rhody
	Plantation State

No state symbol has been more widely used within a state than the anchor at the center of the flag of Rhode Island. It was chosen as the symbol of the colony of Rhode Island and the Providence Plantations at the first Rhode Island General Assembly in 1647. In 1664, a blue scroll with the word "Hope" was added, because the anchor is the Christian symbol of hope. In 1882, 13 gold stars were added, surrounding the two earlier emblems. The flag, its white field taken from the regimental facings of the Rhode Island militia during the Revolution, was adopted in its present form in 1897.

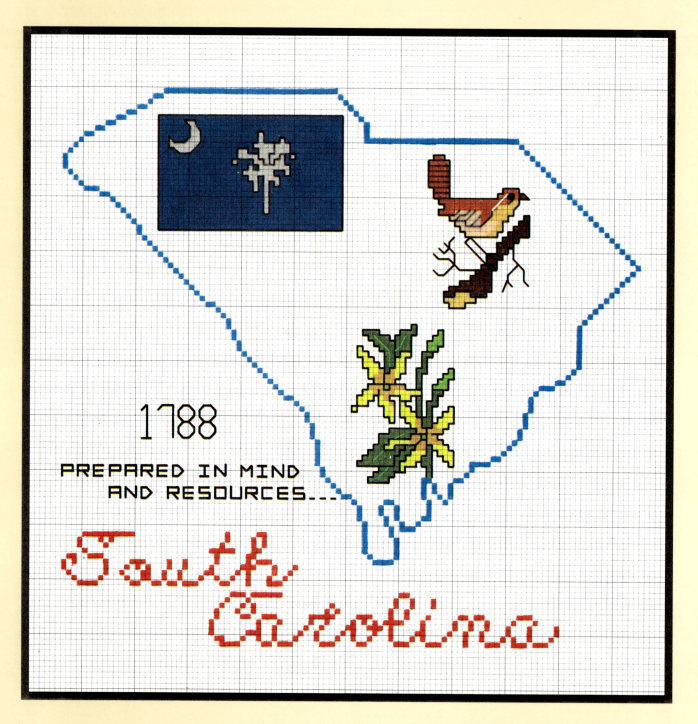

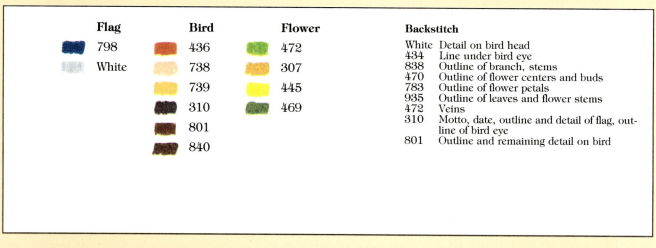

Flag	Bird	Flower	Backstitch	
798	436	472	White	Detail on bird head
White	738	307	434	Line under bird eye
	739	445	838	Outline of branch, stems
	310	469	470	Outline of flower centers and buds
	801		783	Outline of flower petals
	840		935	Outline of leaves and flower stems
			472	Veins
			310	Motto, date, outline and detail of flag, outline of bird eye
			801	Outline and remaining detail on bird

SOUTH CAROLINA

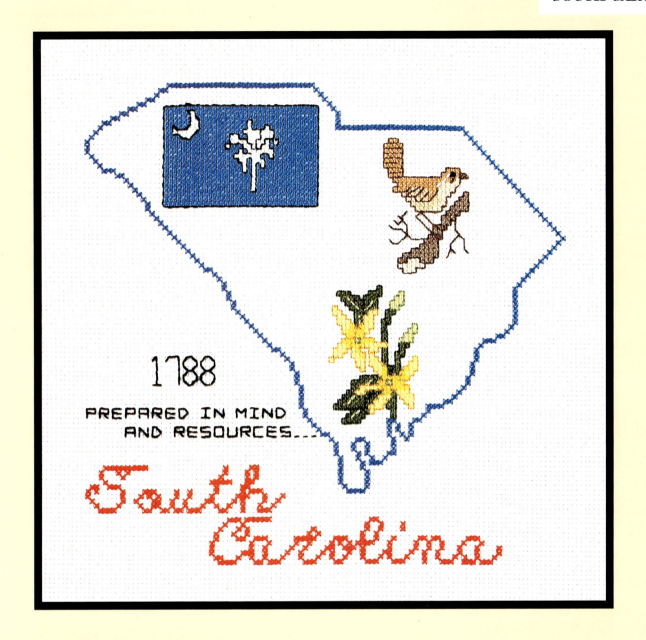

Entered Union:	May 23, 1788
	8th state
Bird:	Carolina wren
Flower:	Carolina yellow jessamine
Nickname:	The Palmetto State

A silver crescent and a silver palmetto stand strong and unadorned on the blue field of the state flag of South Carolina. Both symbols date from the American Revolution, and the symbols and the flag survived both the state's entry into the Confederacy and its return to the Union. In 1775, Colonel William Moultrie designed a silver crescent bearing the legend "Liberty or Death" as a device for the tall blue caps of his South Carolina militia.

On June 28, 1779, nine British warships laid seige to the ramshackle American fort on Sullivan Island in Charleston Harbor. Early in the battle, the fort's flagstaff was shattered by British shot and immediately replaced by a palmetto staff, which, like the fort, endured the battle unbroken. The spongy palmetto logs of which the fort was built repelled the British cannonballs, which simply bounced off the walls. During the night, three of the attacking British frigates ran aground and the other six stole away. The British never again attempted to take Charleston Harbor.

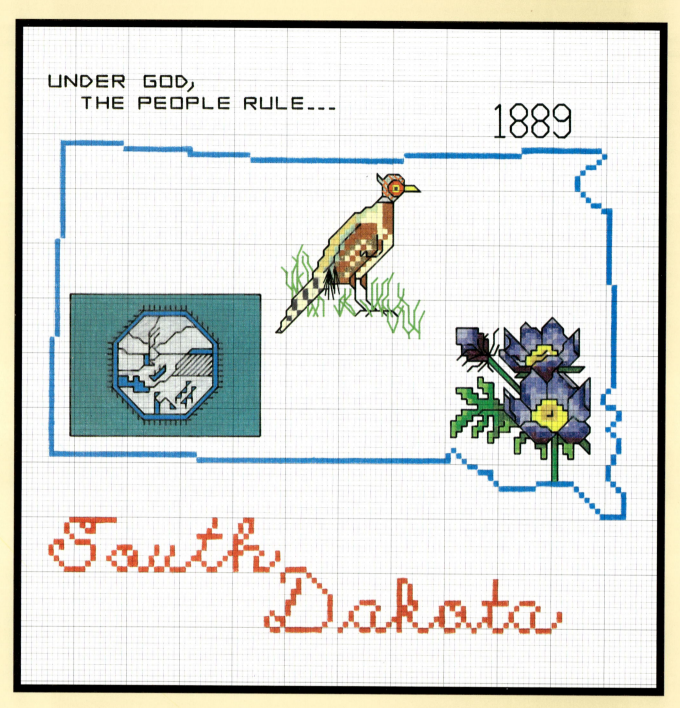

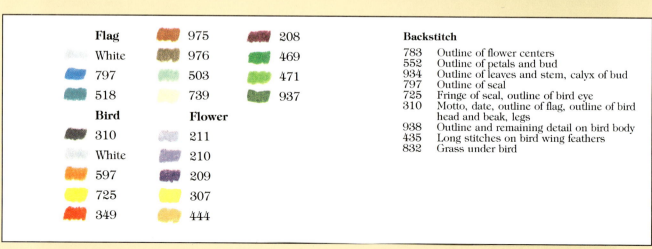

SOUTH DAKOTA

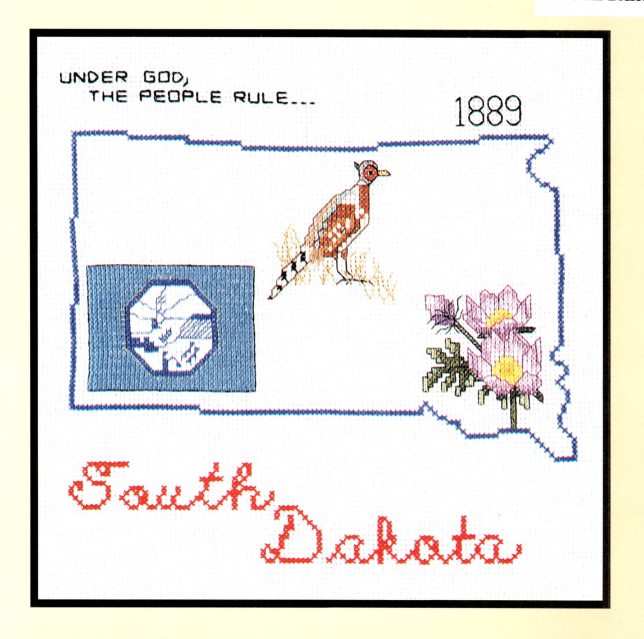

Entered Union:	November 2, 1889
	40th state
Bird:	Ring-necked pheasant
Flower:	American pasque flower
Nicknames:	Sunshine State
	Coyote State
	Land of Infinite Variety

South Dakota's state flag stakes her claim as the Sunshine State, against all comers, with a blazing golden sun on a field of sky blue. The state seal is bisected by an image of the broad Missouri River—with the ubiquitous steamboat. Pictured on the far bank of the river, are a smelting chimney and factory buildings, and, in the foreground, a plain with stacked wheat, a herd of cattle, and a farmer plowing complete the scene.

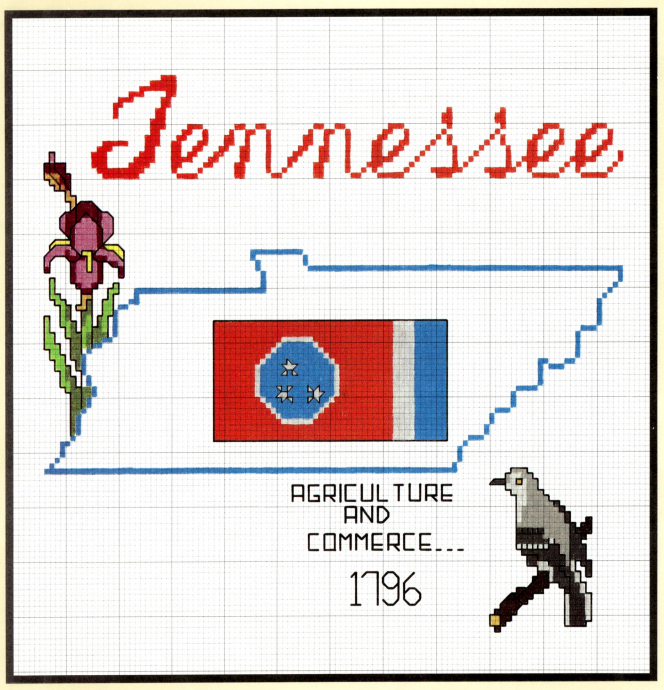

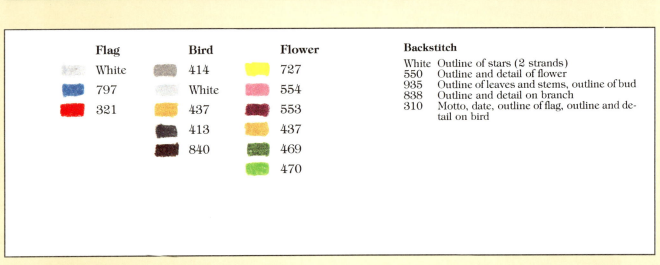

Flag	Bird	Flower
White	414	727
797	White	554
321	437	553
	413	437
	840	469
		470

Backstitch

White Outline of stars (2 strands)
550 Outline and detail of flower
935 Outline of leaves and stems, outline of bud
838 Outline and detail on branch
310 Motto, date, outline of flag, outline and detail on bird

TENNESSEE

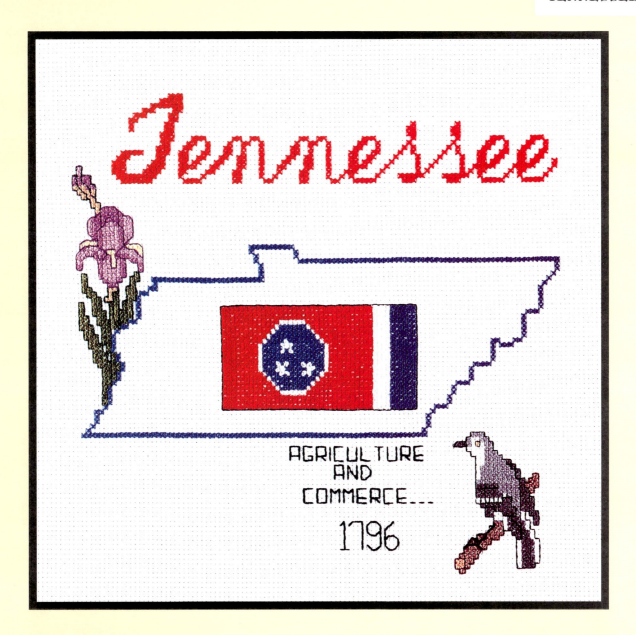

Entered Union:	June 1, 1796
	16th state
Bird:	Mockingbird
Flower:	Iris
Nickname:	The Volunteer State

Tennessee was the third state admitted to the Union after the original 13, and the three white stars in a blue disc, rimmed in white, at the center of the red state flag, stand for this and more. A broad state, over 400 miles across, Tennessee has three grand divisions determined by her varied topography: her eastern mountains, among the highest in the Appalachians; her rolling valleys and plains; and her flood-plain bottomland bordering the Mississippi River. Tennessee has given the Union three presidents: Andrew Jackson, James K. Polk, and Andrew Johnson. At the fly end of the state flag, a narrow vertical strip of white and a broader vertical band of blue add color when the flag hangs without wind.

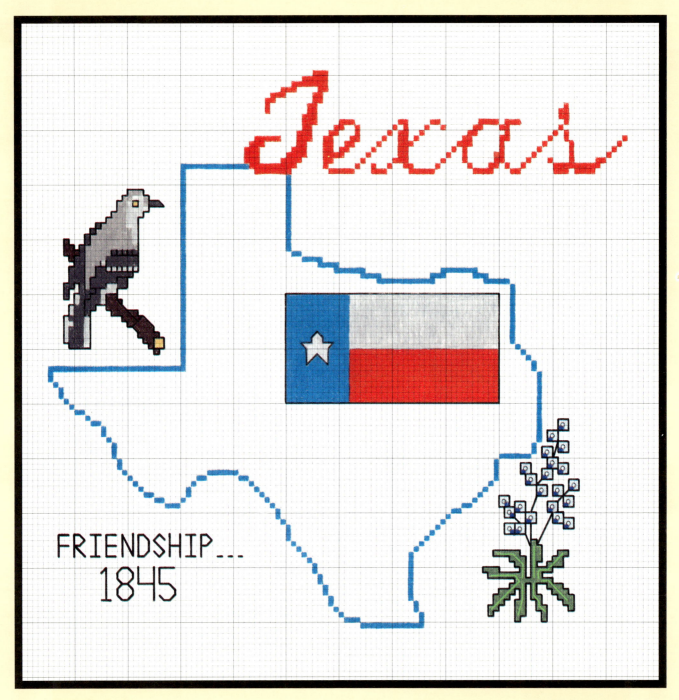

Flag	Bird	Flower	Back stitch	
White	414	334	White	Outline of star
321	White	312	744	French knot flower centers
797	437	469	937	Outline of leaves, long stitch stems
	413		471	Veins
	840		336	Outline of flowers
			838	Outline of branch
			310	Outline of flag, outline and detail on bird

TEXAS

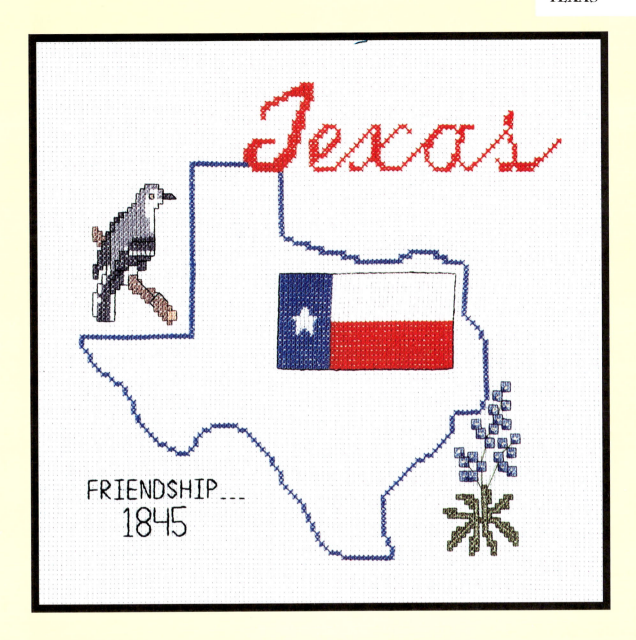

Entered Union: December 29, 1845
28th state
Bird: Mockingbird
Flower: Bluebonnet
Nickname: Lone Star State

In 1519 the Spanish sea captain, Pineda, mapped the Texas coastline. In 1528 shipwrecked Spaniards moved inland from Galveston Island and traveled all the way to the Pacific. The Spanish and French vied for dominance of the territory until 1821 when Texas became a Mexican state.

In 1836, the Texas Republic proclaimed its independence from Mexico. After the famous massacres at the Alamo and at Goliad, General Sam Houston's Texas army routed the Mexican forces and captured Santa Anna at the decisive Battle of San Jacinto. The new republic remained independent until 1845, when its people voted to join the Union as the 28th state.

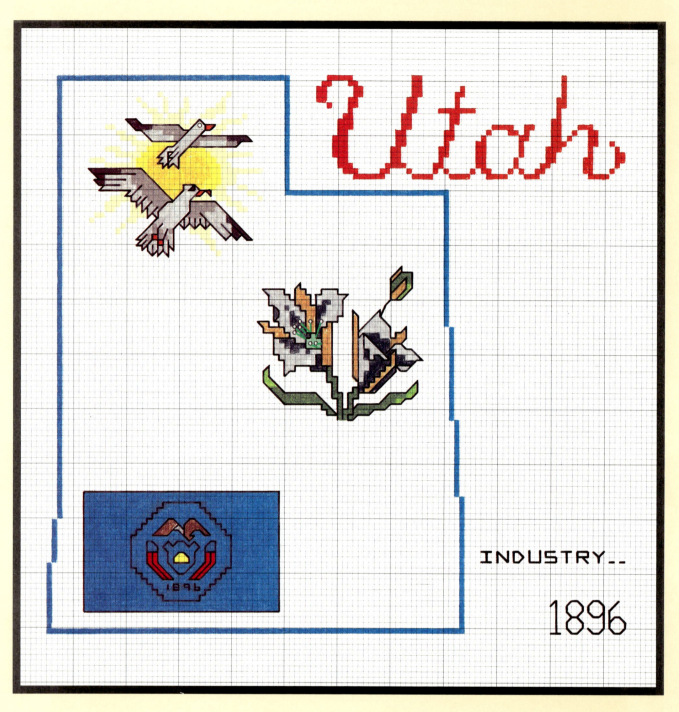

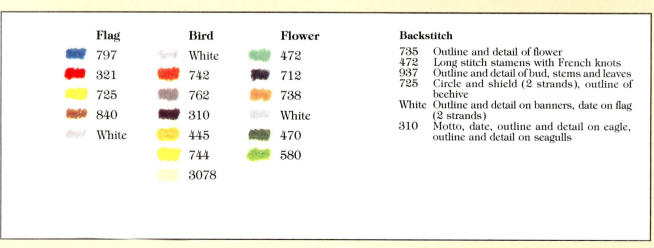

Flag	Bird	Flower	Backstitch	
797	White	472	735	Outline and detail of flower
321	742	712	472	Long stitch stamens with French knots
725	762	738	937	Outline and detail of bud, stems and leaves
840	310	White	725	Circle and shield (2 strands), outline of beehive
White	445	470	White	Outline and detail on banners, date on flag (2 strands)
	744	580	310	Motto, date, outline and detail on eagle, outline and detail on seagulls
	3078			

UTAH

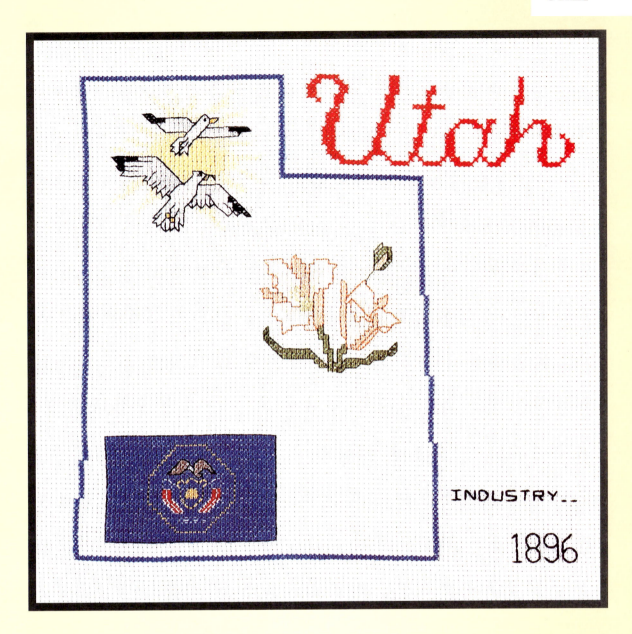

Entered Union:	January 4, 1896
	45th state
Bird:	Seagull
Flower:	Sego lily
Nickname:	Beehive State

Utah's state flag shows abundant evidence of the state's Mormon heritage. On a blue field, surmounted by an American eagle and flanked by dual Stars and Stripes, a beehive rests within sprigs of sego lily, the roots of which were eaten by the early Mormon settlers during periods of hardship. The word *Deseret* that appears on the state flag is from the Book of Mormon; it means "honeybee." The word "Industry" also appears, as does the year of the first Mormon settlement, 1847, and the year Utah attained statehood, 1898.

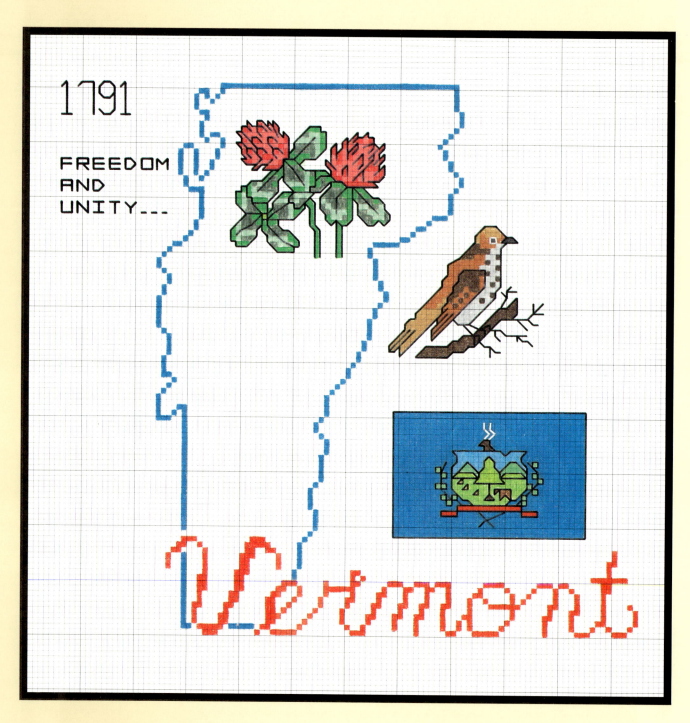

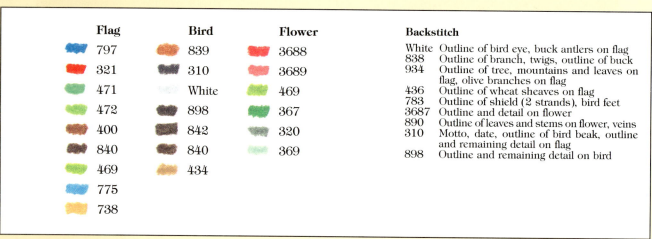

Flag	Bird	Flower	Backstitch	
797	839	3688	White	Outline of bird eye, buck antlers on flag
321	310	3689	838	Outline of branch, twigs, outline of buck
471	White	469	934	Outline of tree, mountains and leaves on flag, olive branches on flag
472	898	367	436	Outline of wheat sheaves on flag
400	842	320	783	Outline of shield (2 strands), bird feet
840	840	369	3687	Outline and detail on flower
469	434		890	Outline of leaves and stems on flower, veins
775			310	Motto, date, outline of bird beak, outline and remaining detail on flag
738			898	Outline and remaining detail on bird

VERMONT

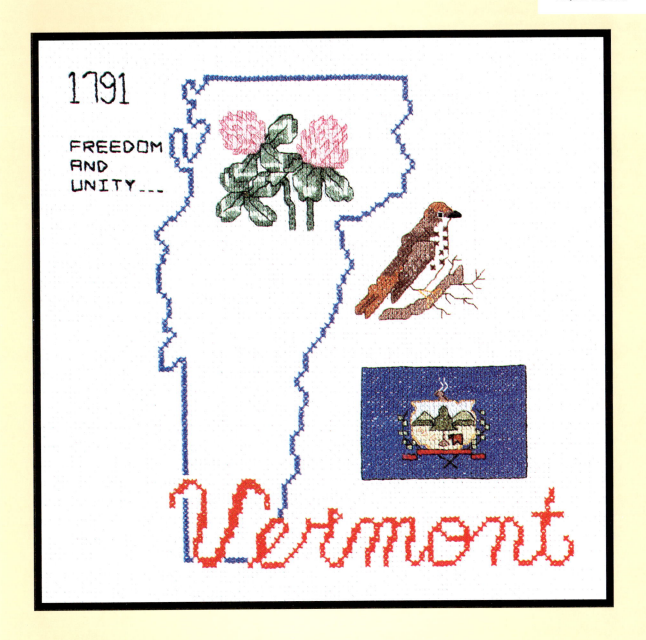

Entered Union: March 4, 1791
14th state
Bird: Hermit thrush
Flower: Red clover
Nickname: Green Mountain State

At the Battle of Bennington, in 1777, in what was then New Hampshire but later that same year became Vermont, the Stars and Stripes were first carried into battle. Thus it is that New Hampshire claims to be the first state to fly the Stars and Stripes—but in 1777, Vermont claimed her own independence from New Hampshire and, four years later, entered the Union.

Beneath a stag's head crest, the shield of the flag of Vermont pictures a cow peacefully at rest beneath a magnificent evergreen tree, with sheaves of wheat at the side and the Green Mountains in the distance. The two crossed pine boughs that spring from the base of the shield commemorate the pine badges worn by Vermonters at the Battle of Plattsburgh in 1814.

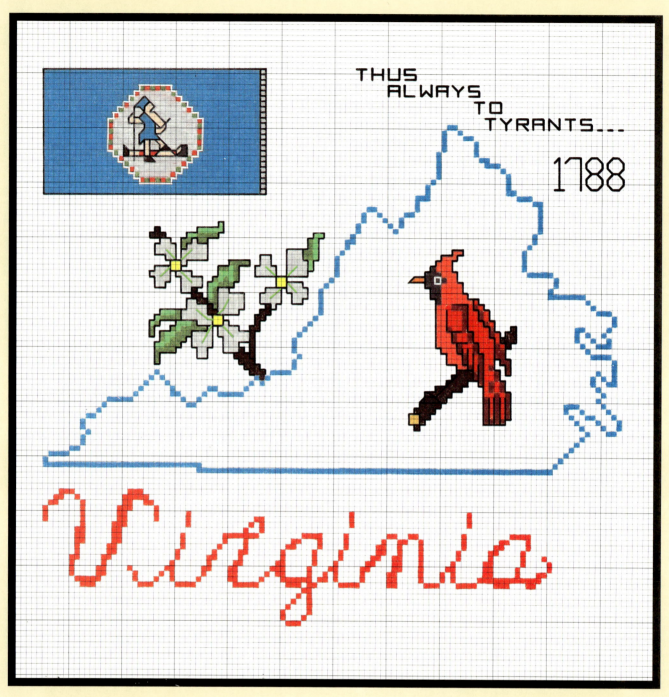

VIRGINIA

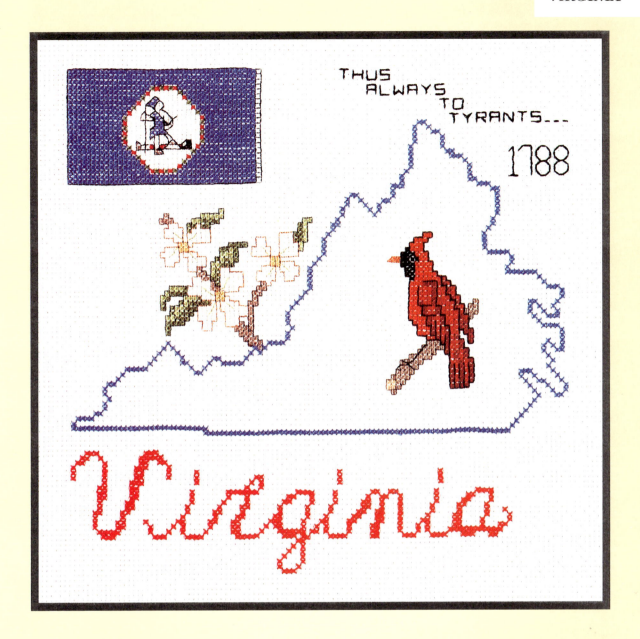

Entered Union: June 26, 1788
10th state
Bird: Cardinal
Flower: American dogwood
Nicknames: Old Dominion State
Mother of Presidents
Cavalier State

The shield of the state flag of Virginia, designed in 1776, was also displayed on flags of that state during the Civil War. Virtue, pictured as an Amazon, with a sheathed sword cradled in her left arm and a spear held point down in her right hand, treads on the figure of Tyranny, who has lost his crown and who holds a scourge and a broken chain. The shield is surrounded by a garland of red, green, and gold vegetation.

Virginia is called the Mother of Presidents, not only because she has provided the greatest number of them, but they are among the greatest: Washington, Jefferson, Madison, Monroe, Harrison, Tyler, and Zachary Taylor.

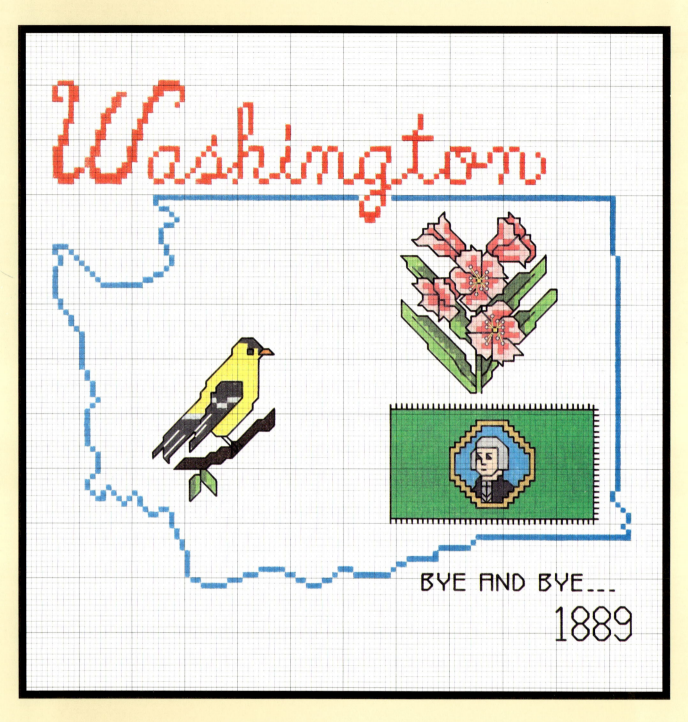
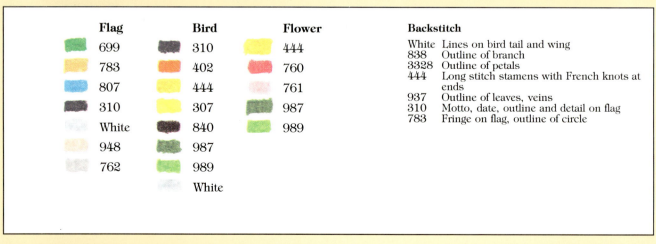

WASHINGTON

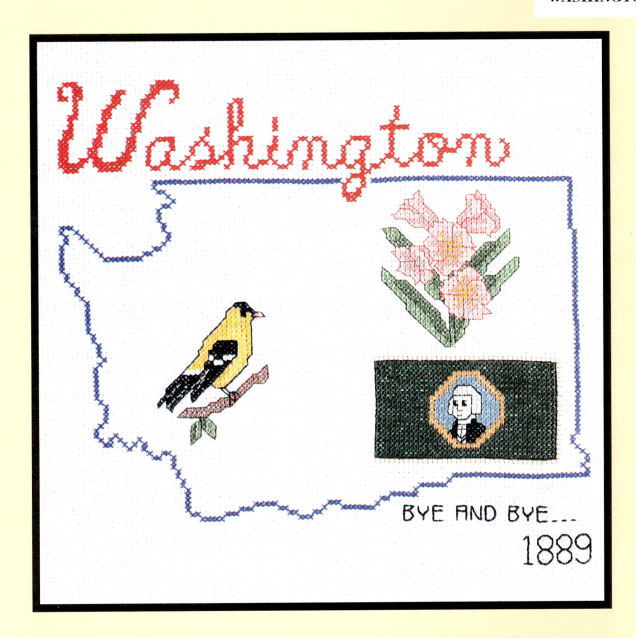

Entered Union:	November 11, 1889
	42nd state
Bird:	Willow goldfinch
Flower:	Rhododendron
Nicknames:	Evergreen State
	Chinook State

There is no ambiguity in the meaning of the flag of the state of Washington. When he was presented with the new Washington state seal for adaptation to a state flag, Olympia jeweler Charles Talcott took one look at the seal containing a covered wagon, a sailing vessel, Mount Rainier, wheat, sheep, the port of Tacoma, and, yes, a steamboat—and pronounced it too complicated. Using an ink bottle and a silver dollar, Talcott traced two concentric circles and placed a postage stamp bearing the image of George Washington at the center, on a striking green field. This basic design has remained the same ever since.

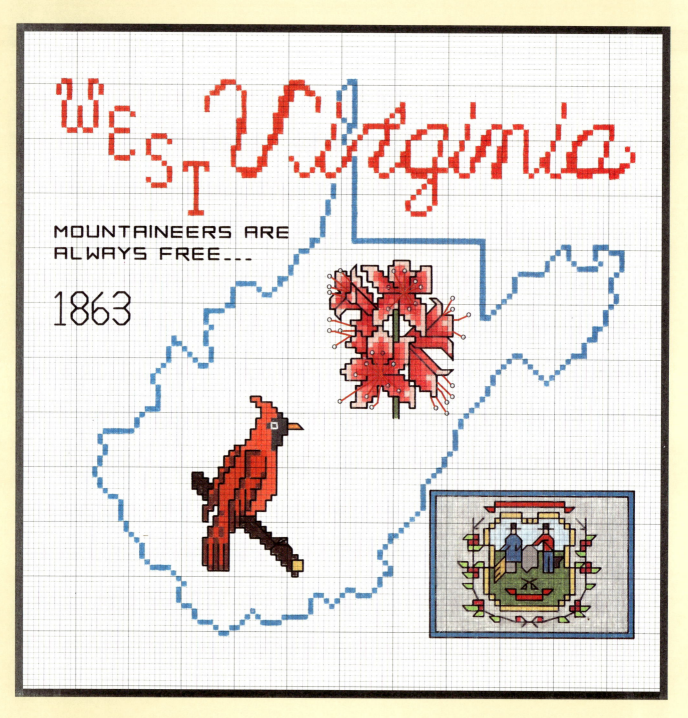

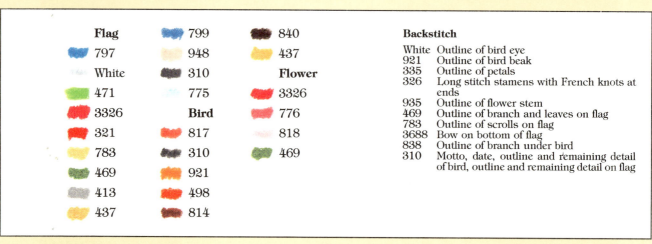

WEST VIRGINIA

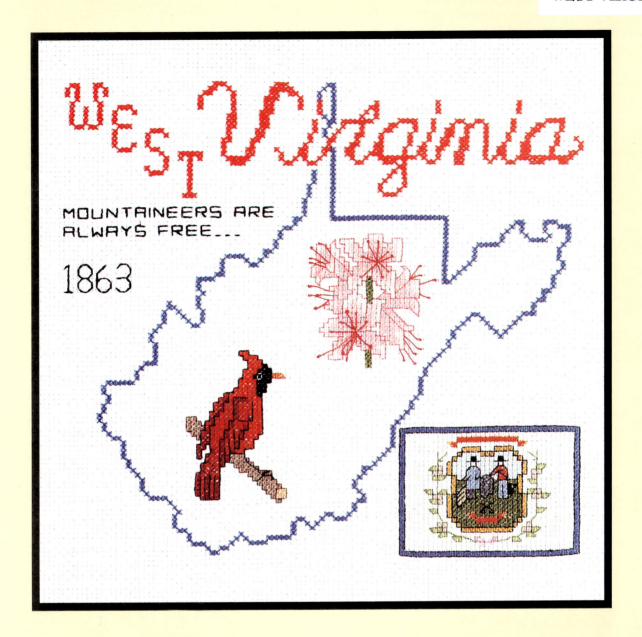

Entered State:	June 20, 1863
	35th state
Bird:	Cardinal
Flower:	Rhododendron
Nicknames:	Mountain State
	Panhandle State

The flag of West Virginia shows two peaceful West Virginians—a farmer and a miner—flanking a rough-hewn stone that bears the date 1863, the year of the state's entry into the Union, on a broad white field, with a wide blue border. Blossoming garlands of rhododendron are tied at the center with a rose-colored ribbon. West Virginia's statehood, coming as it did in the midst of the Civil War, amplifies the meaning of her motto, *Montan Semper Libri*—"Mountaineers Are Always Free Men."

Flag	Bird		Backstitch	
797	310	840	White	Outline of bird eye, outline of blue banner on flag, lines in small circle
334	844	469	783	Outline of flag and shield, fringe, line above blue banner (2 strands)
White	White	648	550	Outline of petals
310	922	**Flower**	444	French knot flower centers
840	920	554	838	Outline of branch
321	645	553	934	Outline of leaves, veins and stems
948	646	470	310	Motto, date, outline and remaining detail on bird, remaining detail on flag
725		469		
469				

WISCONSIN

Entered Union: May 29, 1848
30th state
Bird: Robin
Flower: Violet
Nicknames: Badger State
America's Dairyland

Wisconsin's flag bears the arms of the state on a gold-fringed blue ground that indicates its regimental origins. Crested by the native badger and bearing the slogan, "Forward," on a white banner, the state shield is supported by the image of a sailor in 1848 naval uniform on one side and by that of a miner with his pick on the other.

The shield itself is divided into four quarters containing, respectively, a plow, an anchor, a crossed pick and shovel, and a muscular forearm. Superimposed on the four sections is the shield of the United States. A cornucopia, a pig-lead ingot, and 13 stars at the base complete the device. Wisconsin takes its nickname, Badger State, from the history of its early miners, whose burrow-like huts resembled badger holes.

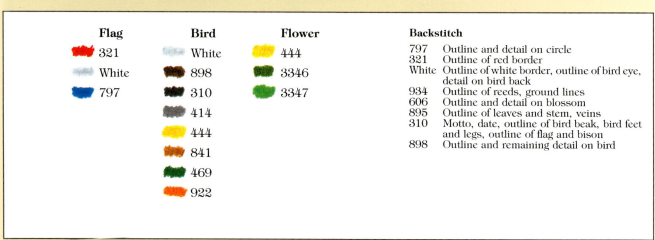

Flag	Bird	Flower	Backstitch	
321	White	444	797	Outline and detail on circle
White	898	3346	321	Outline of red border
797	310	3347	White	Outline of white border, outline of bird eye, detail on bird back
	414		934	Outline of reeds, ground lines
	444		606	Outline and detail on blossom
	841		895	Outline of leaves and stem, veins
	469		310	Motto, date, outline of bird beak, bird feet and legs, outline of flag and bison
	922		898	Outline and remaining detail on bird

WYOMING

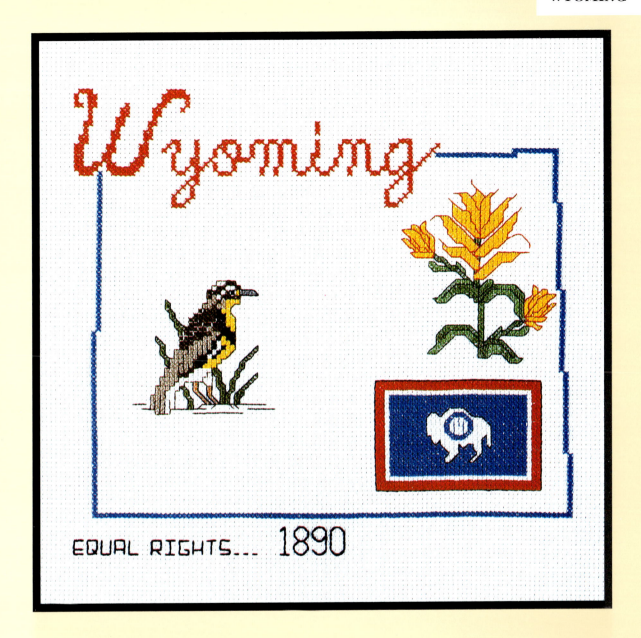

Entered Union: July 11, 1890
44th state
Bird: Meadowlark
Flower: Indian paintbrush
Nicknames: Cowboy State
Equality State
Sagebrush State
Wonderful Wyoming

A silhouetted white bison stands on a rectangular blue field, surrounded alternately by white and red borders, on Wyoming's state flag. Within the bison silhouette is the blue state seal of Wyoming, where a cowboy and a miner are shown flanking a female winged Victory, who bears the slogan, "Equal Rights." In 1924, Wyoming elected the first woman governor in the United States. The three figures on the Wyoming shield stand upon the shield of the United States.

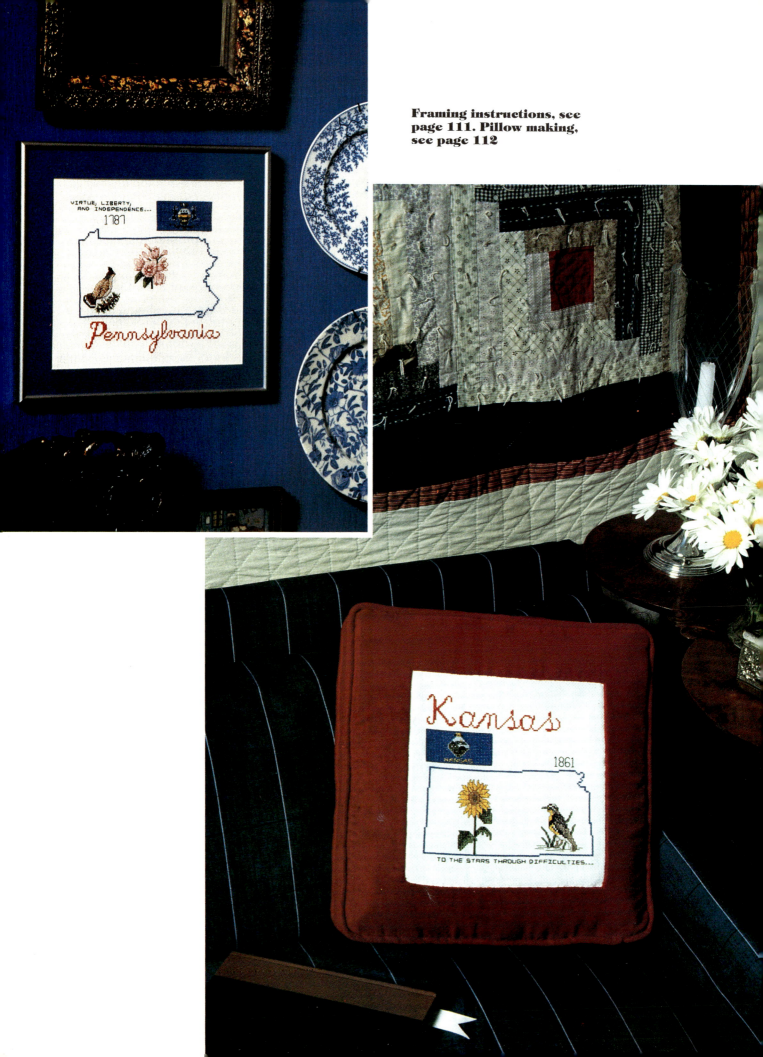

Framing instructions, see page 111. Pillow making, see page 112

FINISHING

If you have been careful while working, your embroidery may not need washing before ironing. If, however, the piece is soiled, special care must be taken in washing.

Always wash each piece separately. First, soak the piece in cold water and white vinegar for a half hour, then wash it in lukewarm water and mild, pure soap. DO NOT use Woolite™, detergents, or chlorine bleach. Rinse several times in clear water. Do not worry if water becomes colored when washing—continue rinsing in clear water. Roll the embroidery between two clean towels squeezing gently without wringing. DO NOT allow embroidered piece to touch upon itself. Unroll towels and spread piece outflat to dry on a towel. NEVER leave damp embroidery folded or in a heap.

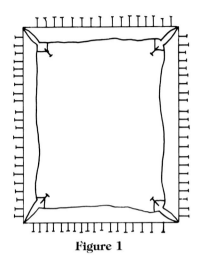

Figure 1

To iron, place the dry embroidery face down between two clean towels and press with a warm—not hot—iron. To remove creases or folds, you may find it necessary to use the steam setting on your iron.

Do not use Scotchgard™ or other such products on your embroidery, since they can cause dyes to run or fade. Drycleaning is not recommended either since cleaning chemicals can also react with thread dyes.

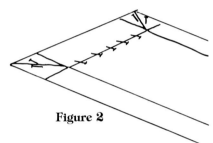

Figure 2

MOUNTING AND FRAMING

Before taking your embroidery to a professional framer or framing the piece yourself, it should be mounted. Cut mat board to desired size. Place embroidery right side down on a flat surface. center mat board squarely on piece, following the weave of the fabric for straight edge. Pin fabric to board (Figure 1), folding fabric over board and mitering corners (Figure 2). With white thread, whipstitch mitered corners (Figure 3). With buttonhole twist or other heavy thread, lace back and forth pulling stitches to keep embroidery taut (Figures 4 and 5). Embroidery is now ready for framing.

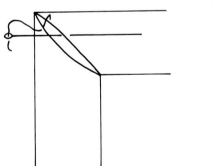

Figure 3

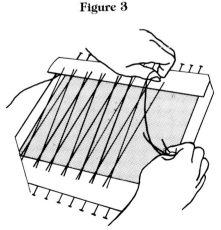

Figure 4

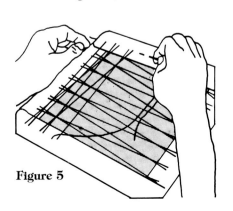

Figure 5

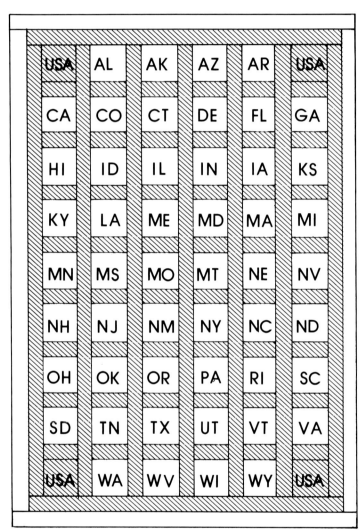

Figure 6

PILLOW INSTRUCTIONS

MATERIALS: Embroidered square on 14-count fabric. 1 yd velvet, corduroy, or other sturdy fabric. 14" pillow form with 2" edges. 12" zipper. 3 yds. cording.

TO CUT: Cut 2 squares, 14" by 14". Cut strip 5" by 45" and 2 strips 3½" by 13".

TO ASSEMBLE: Baste 13" strips together allowing ¾" seam to form 5" by 13" piece for zipper. Sew zipper into seam. Sew this piece to end of 45" strip. Cut cord in half. Fold long edges of strip over cord, leaving 2" of fabric at middle of strip. With zipper foot, sew cording in place along edges of strip leaving ½" seam allowance. Cut 9½" square "window" in center of one 14" square. Slash corners ⅜". Center embroidery in window, using weave of fabric to ensure that it is straight. From right side, whipstitch carefully in place, turning under ½" edge on raw edge of window. Placing zipper placket at bottom, pin gusset in place around pillow top. Trim extra fabric and sew ends of gusset together. Sew pillow top and gusset together. Pin pillow back in place. Open zipper. Sew pillow back in place. Trim seams.

QUILT INSTRUCTIONS

SIZE: Quilt is approximately 78" by 114".

MATERIALS: 5¾ yds. 14-count aida cloth for embroidery; 3¼ yds. blue cotton fabric for sashing or lattice strips and corners; ¾ yds. red cotton fabric for borders; 7 yds. cotton for backing; 1 yd. cotton for binding; 90" by 120" batting.

TO CUT BLOCKS AND BORDERS: Trim off selvages. Wash and iron cottons. For embroidery, cut 50 12" squares. Work embroidery, wash and press, following instructions above. For quilt, embroidered squares must be cut down to 10½". To cut squares accurately, measure from the center of the design to each of the 4 sides, i.e., from center to top, 5¼", from center to bottom, 5¼", and from center to each edge, 5¼". From blue fabric, cut 7 strips, 2½" by 108"; 2 strips, 2½" by 76"; 4 corner blocks, 10½" by 10½"; and 48 strips, 2½" by 10½". Piece red fabric to make 2 strips, 2½" by 80"; and 2 strips, 2½" by 112". From backing fabric, cut 2 strips, 42" by 3½ yds. Cut binding fabric in 2" bias strips and piece together to about 390" long.

TO ASSEMBLE: Following Figure 6, arrange the blocks and strips on a large, flat surface. Allowing ¼" for seams throughout, sew blocks and short strips together in vertical rows. Taking care to align blocks horizontally, join rows together with blue strip between, then sew blue strip to each side. Trim top and bottom edges. Sew blue strip to top and bottom; trim ends. Seam red border to sides, then to top and bottom.

Stitch the two backing lengths together and press seams open. Lay flat with wrong side up. Seams run the length of the quilt. Spread batting on top of backing. Center the quilt top on the batting and backing. Secure all three layers together, working from the center outward. You may use long running stitches. First, baste diagonally from center to corners then from top to bottom; right to left, OR you may use safety pins, pinning 4" apart from the center outward. Check backing and remove all wrinkles.

You may quilt any design in the borders and strips. Use the USA outline (Figure 7) for the 4 plain blocks and quilt around each state outline in the state blocks.

Sew bias binding to all edges. Trim excess backing fabric and batting to match edge of quilt top. Turn binding to wrong side, turn under raw edge, and sew in place.

RESOURCES

DMC Embroidery Floss can be obtained from:
The DMC Corporation
107 Trumbull Street
Elizabeth, N. J. 07206

Aida cloth can be ordered from:
Hansi's House
35 Fairfield Place
West Caldwell, N. J. 07006

STRAIGHT OF GOODS

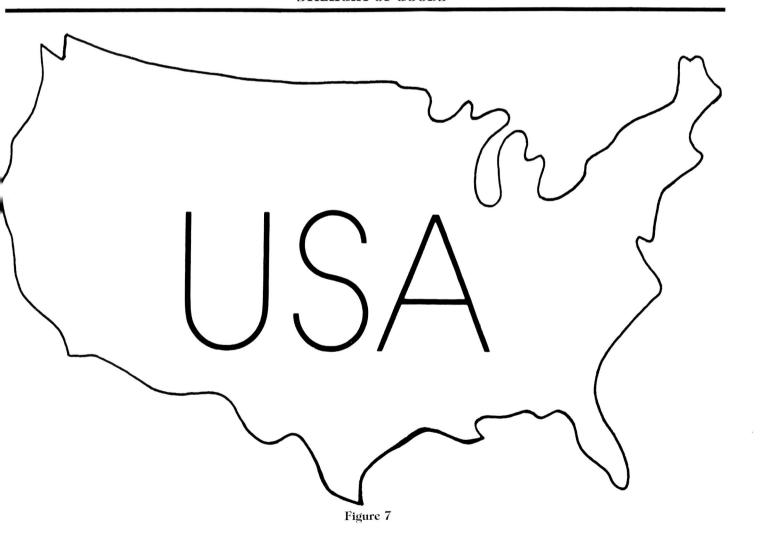

Figure 7